General Editor:	David Jollands
Design Director:	Elwyn Blacker
Consultant Authors:	Paul Doherty
	Roy Edwards
	Alan Hibbert
	Jim Hudson
	John Little
	John Mason
	Cleland McVeigh
	Peter Metcalfe
	Beverley Moody
	Patrick Moore
	Michael Pollard
	Keith Porter
	Tim Pridgeon
	Derek Slack
	Ian Soden
	Tony Soper
	Alan Thomas
Research Editor:	Simon Jollands
Design and Production:	BLA Publishing Limited
	Michael Blacker
	Simon Blacker
	Margaret Hickey
	Alison Lawrenson
	Graeme Little
	David Oakley
	Lorrie Spooner
Artists:	Paul Doherty
	John Flynn/Linden Artists
	Hayward & Martin
	Richard Lewis
	Steve Lings/Linden Artists
	Jane Pickering/Linden Artists
	Chris Rotheroe/Linden Artists
	Eric Thomas
	Brian Watson/Linden Artists
	Phil Weare/Linden Artists
	Rosie Vane-Wright

CAMBRIDGE SCIENCE UNIVERSE

MACHINES, POWER & TRANSPORT

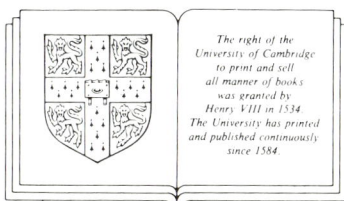

The right of the
University of Cambridge
to print and sell
all manner of books
was granted by
Henry VIII in 1534.
The University has printed
and published continuously
since 1584.

CAMBRIDGE UNIVERSITY PRESS

Cambridge · London · New York · New Rochelle · Melbourne · Sydney

Acknowledgements

The publishers wish to thank the following organizations for their invaluable assistance in the preparation of this book.

Airships Industries (UK) Ltd
Austin Rover Group Ltd
British Caledonian
British Hovercraft Corporation Ltd
British Petroleum
British Robot Association
British Telecom
Canon (UK)
Central Electricity Generating Board
Cincinnati Milacron Ltd
Commodore (UK) Ltd
Disabled Living Foundation
Dundee University
Eaton (UK) Ltd
Ferranti plc
Ford Motor Company
Furuno Ltd
General Electrical Company plc
Japan Ship Centre
Kodak Museum
Longines
NASA
National Film Board of Canada
Omega Electronic
Philips International bv
The Plessey Company plc
Rediffusion Simulation Ltd
Rolls-Royce Ltd
Royal Greenwich Observatory
Royal Smeets Offset
Shell
Sony (UK)
Southern Positives and Negatives (SPAN)
Standard Telephones and Cables
United Nations Organization
US Information Service

Published by the Press Syndicate of
the University of Cambridge,
The Pitt Building, Trumpington Street,
Cambridge CB2 1RP
32 East 57th Street, New York, NY 10022, USA
296 Beaconsfield Parade, Middle Park,
Melbourne 3206, Australia

© BLA Publishing Limited 1984

First published 1984

Library of Congress Catalog Card Number: 83-25253

British Library Cataloguing in Publication Data

Cambridge science universe.
Vol. 5: Machines, power and transport
1. Science — Juvenile Literature
I. Jollands, David
500   Q163

ISBN 0-521-26001-9

This book was designed and produced by
BLA Publishing Limited, Swan Court,
East Grinstead, Sussex, England.

Also in LONDON · HONG KONG · TAIPEI · NEW YORK · SINGAPORE

A Ling Kee Company

Phototypeset in Great Britain by
Southern Positives and Negatives (SPAN).
Colour origination by Chris Willcock Reproductions,
Premier Graphics and Planway Ltd.
Printed and bound in The Netherlands by
Royal Smeets Offset BV, Weert.

Photographic credits

t = top   b = bottom   l = left   r = right   c = centre

Cover photographs: *tl* ZEFA: *tc* Elgin Press; *tr, cr, br* ZEFA; *bl* Colorsport.

Title page: ZEFA

4 ZEFA; 5*tl* Michael Holford; 5*c*, 5*r* Philips; 5*b* Cincinnati Milacron Ltd; 7*bl*, 7*tr*, 8 Michael Holford; 10, 12, 14*tr*, 14*bl* ZEFA; 15*t* Mansell Collection; 18 Michael Holford; 19 Mike Williams/National Trust; 20*l*, 20*r*, 21*t*, 21*b* Michael Holford; 21*r* ZEFA; 22*t* Mansell Collection; 22*b*, 25*t*, 27*tl*, 27*tr* The British Engineerium; 27*br*, 28, 29*tl*, 29*r*, 29*cr*, 29*bl* ZEFA; 30*l*, 30*r* Mansell Collection; 31*t* ZEFA; 31*l* Mansell Collection; 31*cr* The British Engineerium; 34*t* Mansell Collection; 34*l* David Spurdens; 35 LAT Photographic Ltd; 36*l* Central Electricity Generating Board; 36*cr*, 37*bl* ZEFA; 37*tr* Japan Ship Centre; 38*t* Mansell Collection; 38*b* ZEFA; 39*t*, 39*b* Airship Industries (UK) Ltd; 40*t*, 40*b*, 41*tl*, 41*tr*, 41*b* Mansell Collection; 43 British Caledonian; 44*t*, 44*b* The Royal Aeronautical Society; 45*t*, 45*l* British Caledonian; 45*c* Rolls-Royce Ltd; 48*bl*, 48*tr*, 49*br*, 50*t* ZEFA; 51*br* British Hovercraft Corporation Ltd; 52*t* Elswick Special Vehicles Ltd; 52*bl*, 53*c* ZEFA; 53*tr* Telesensory Systems Inc; 53*br* Possum Controls Ltd; 54*t* Department of Trade and Industry; 54*b* ZEFA; 55*br* Eaton (UK) Ltd; 56, 61 Cincinnati Milacron Ltd; 56*t* The Austin Rover Group Ltd; 57*tl* Cincinnati Milacron Ltd; 57*br* The Austin Rover Group Ltd; 58*l*, 58*t*, 58*tr* GEC Electrical Projects Ltd; 59*l*, 59*r* The British Robot Association; 60*l* NASA/US Information Service; 60*t* Ferranti plc; 61*t*, 61*b* ZEFA

Contents

NOTE TO THE READER: while you are reading this book you will notice that certain words appear in **bold type**. This is to indicate a word listed in the Glossary on page 62. This glossary gives brief explanations of words which may be new to you.

Introduction

An athlete uses great skill as well as strength, when putting the shot. The versatile human machine is here about to act like a catapult.

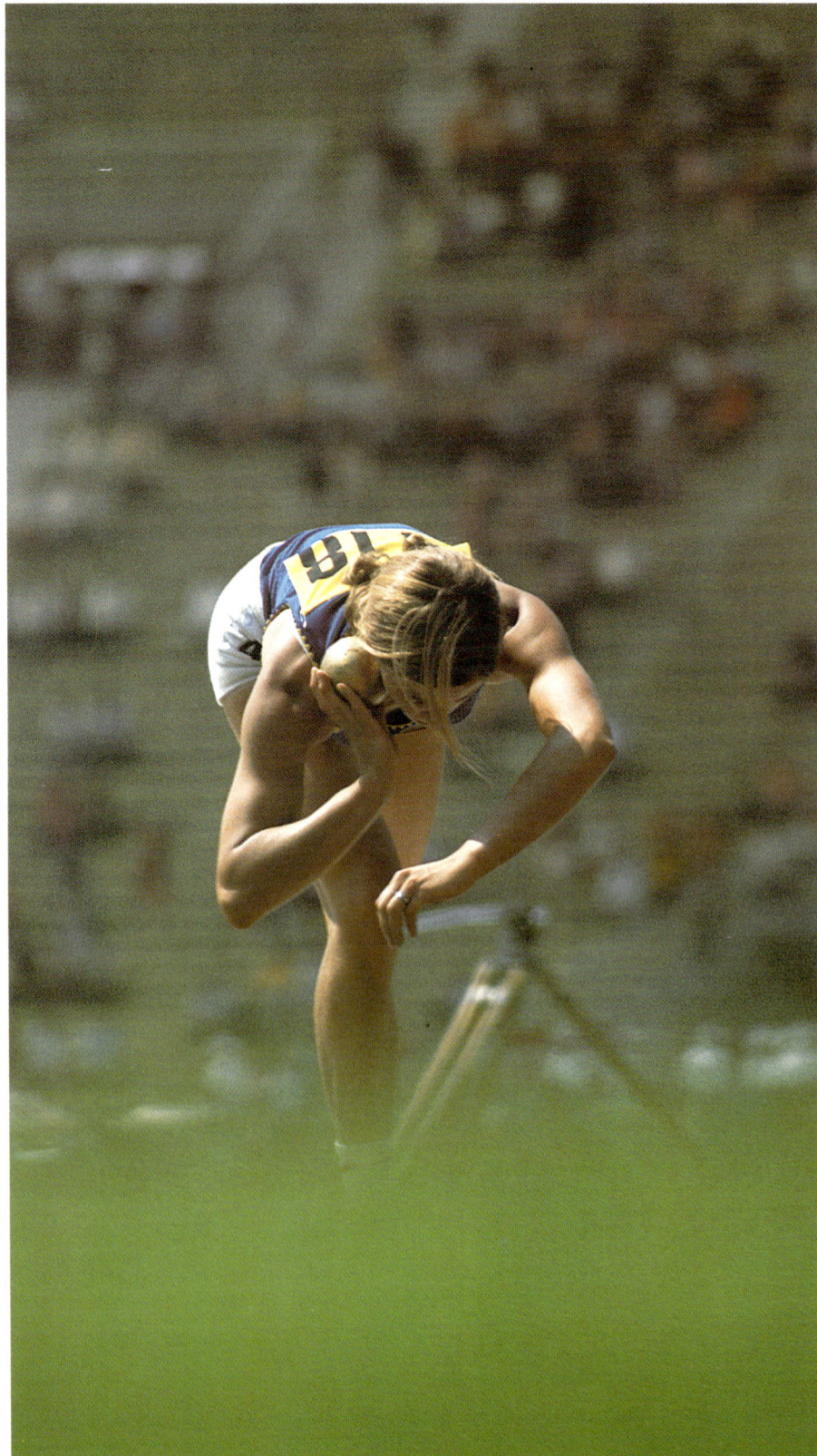

EVERYWHERE WE GO, we are surrounded by **machines**. At home, they do our washing, clean our carpets, dry our hair, and perform all kinds of jobs to save us time and effort. We travel with the help of machines. They enable us to tell the time. They help us build our houses.

Not all machines have **gears** or engines or wheels. An ordinary wood screw is a machine. So are corkscrews, can-openers and nut-crackers. A machine is any device that makes work easier by reducing the **effort** needed. When you use a screwdriver to fix two pieces of wood together, the spiral thread of the screw does some of the work for you.

The first human beings found themselves living in a hostile **environment**. They had to find their own food and make their own clothing and shelter. There were many wild animals which were enemies. Our early ancestors had to invent their own tools and use their wits to enable them to survive.

Parts of the human body work very well as machines. The jaw is a **lever** that enables us to grind up our food so that we can swallow it easily. The human arm is another lever. To pick up an object you stretch out your arm and lift the object by raising your hand. Your hand might move a metre or so if you raise the object above your head. However, the muscles between your elbow and your shoulder which provide the **force** move only a short distance. The lever, your arm, increases the force.

Your fingers, also, act as levers when, for example, you are eating a meal. A tiny movement in the muscles of your hand enables you to hold the spoon or fork. The lever of your arm helps you to carry the food to your mouth. Some handicapped people whose muscles are faulty in some way cannot carry out these movements, or cannot carry them out precisely. Sometimes they are provided with man-made machines to do the work for them.

Because the human body works so well as a machine, many **robots** – machines that imitate human actions – may be compared with metal people. They have arms that can **pivot** at the shoulder, elbow and wrist. They also have pincer-like fingers that can grasp and pinch and twist. The human body turned out to be a perfect model for the robot-builders. But robots can do many things better than people. They

An early form of mechanical clock designed by Galileo. It was built by his son in 1649. Movement of the pendulum drove a system of cogs which in turn rotated the hand.

Modern car production lines *(bottom)* now use robots for many of the assembly jobs. Note the absence of people in this picture.

This highly advanced system uses a computer, a robot, video equipment and an X-ray tube. With these, iron castings are inspected for flaws and cracks invisible to the human eye.

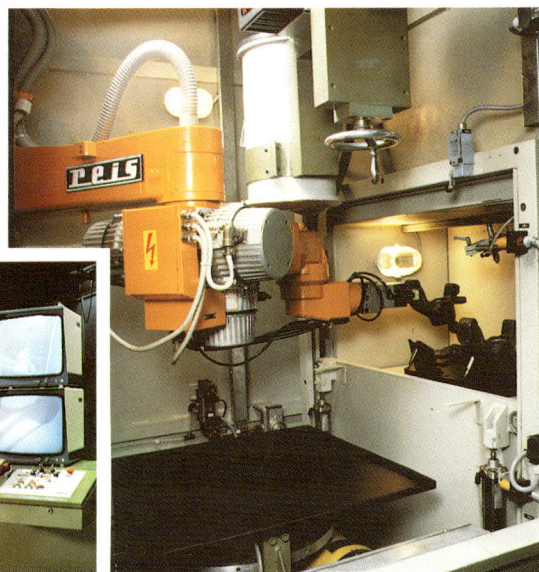

can make more precise movements, and they can handle such things as white-hot metal or poisonous chemicals that would be dangerous for humans.

We use the machines in our bodies – our arms and legs, fingers, jaws, and all the others – when our brains send them signals. The signals travel through the body's nervous system. Robots work in a similar way. They do not have brains, of course – they have computers instead. The computers are **programmed** to perform a series of tasks. On a car production line, for instance, there may be a number of robots. Each one is programmed to do different jobs as the half-finished car passes by on the moving track. One might drill holes in a door-frame and fit hinges. The next might put the door on the hinges. The next might put the handle on the door, and so on until, at the end of the track, the finished car comes off the production line.

Robots are among the latest kinds of machine that humans have invented. They represent the latest chapter in a story that stretches back to the beginning of human life on earth. Human beings have always wanted to do their work better, or faster, or with less effort. They have made use of machines to achieve these aims. Without the help of machines, much of this work would be impossible. A nail is quite a good way of fixing pieces of wood together, but a screw is better. A bicycle is a machine that enables people to travel faster than they could if they were walking. A **pulley** system raises loads with less effort than simple human force.

This book tells the story of how humans developed from their use of the first primitive tools to invent the great variety of complicated machines that surround us today.

The first machines

FOR THE VERY BEGINNING of our story we have to go back about 25 million years. One of the animals inhabiting the Earth then was an ape-like form called *Dryopithecus*. Scientists think *Dryopithecus* was more skilled than any previous ape-like animal. It could swing from branch to branch, grasping them with its hands, and it could also stand up on two legs. This left its hands free.

The ability to stand up on two legs is important, because it leaves the hands free to perform tasks with the use of implements. When species developed which could stand and move easily on two legs, it became possible to use tools. About two million years ago there existed an early human ancestor called *Homo habilis*. This ancestor could use simple stone tools such as rock hammers. For well over a million years after this, the story of human development is about the improvement of stone tools and the invention of new types. It is also about the discovery of new ways of using these tools.

Simple though they were, these early tools greatly increased human chances of surviving in a difficult environment. With a stone axe, our ancestors could chop down small trees. With a stone spearhead they could protect themselves from enemies and hunt for food. With a sharp scraping tool made by chipping pieces off a **flint**, they could clean the insides of

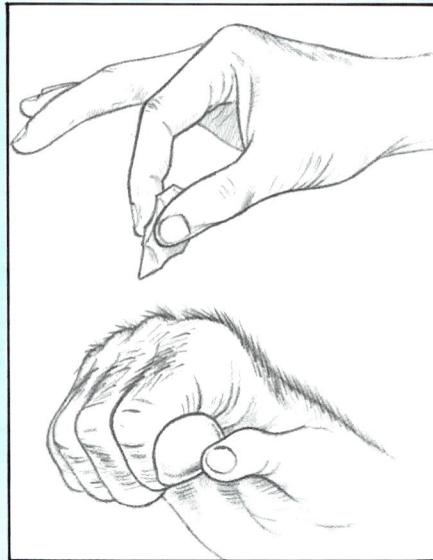

There are two basic grips that hands can perform, the power grip and the precision grip. The human precision grip, shown here, sets us apart from the apes, which have short, clumsy thumbs. The longer, human thumb is able to meet the tips of the other fingers. This gives much finer control and touch, enabling tools to be made and handled with precision.

In the early Stone Age, our human ancestors used stones as tools for scraping and cutting. With these, they could scrape the inner part of animal skins to make clothing. They could also cut and shape branches and fit them with small, sharp flints to make spears. They used these to protect themselves, and to hunt animals for food. They used fire for warmth and protection, and for cooking their food.

animal skins. They could then use these skins for clothing. Using a branch chopped from one of the trees they had felled, our ancestors learned how to make bows and arrows. The arrows were probably tipped with small, sharp chips of flint. The bow and arrow is a more accurate weapon than a spear, and the arrow flies faster and further. It is a more efficient hunting tool.

Hunting was very important to our early ancestors. They did not know how to keep animals for their meat, or how to grow plants for food. They were also threatened by a large number of enemies, including mammoths, rhinoceros, lions, bears and bison. So the invention of hunting weapons gave them an easier, less dangerous life.

About half a million years ago, our ancestors were expert at working with stone to produce sharp cutting edges. They had discovered fire, probably by observing forest fires and taking burning branches from them. They had found that the flames of a fire frightened animals away. They also made another important discovery. They found that if they cooked the meat of the animals they killed, it became tender. This must have been very welcome. It meant there was more food to go round, because even the tougher meat could be made good to eat by cooking for a long time.

The earliest tools made by humans were crude stone axes. Later, the shape of these hand axes was improved by hammering them against other stones.

These harpoons, from the middle Stone Age, were made from antlers. The sharp, backward-sloping teeth clung to the flesh of the animal, preventing its escape.

The animals they killed provided them with another source of material for making tools – bone. Like stone, it could be sharpened. It could be cut into lengths and shaped. Even the smaller bones could be put to use, and it was these that provided a new kind of tool, the needle. Now, instead of roughly hacking furs and hides into shape and wearing them rather like cloaks, it was possible to make warmer clothes which fitted more closely to the shape of the body.

One of the animals that was present in some parts of the world at this time was the reindeer. Its meat was good, and its skin was useful for clothes. It also had antlers, and these probably became the first tools our ancestors used to scrape away at the ground and cultivate it to grow food. It may also have been the branches of the reindeer's antlers that gave humans the idea of making harpoons. Hunting with a spear or with arrows was often disappointing. A wounded animal, mad with pain, could twist away from a spearhead or run away with the arrow. Harpoons have backward-sloping teeth called barbs. These cling to the animal's flesh and prevent it from escaping.

About 30000 years ago the Earth entered an Ice Age. At this time, sheets of ice stretched from the North Pole to cover part of North America and part of Europe all the year round. Our ancestors sheltered from the cold in caves. We now know about the first real machine that was ever invented, because of a painting left on the walls of one of these caves. It was a machine for trapping mammoths instead of hunting them. The trap could be set and would do its work while its inventor was doing something else, or sleeping. Now these first humans were really beginning to find out how to use the materials around them.

The lever and the wheel

If you filled a large box with earth and tried to carry it across the garden, you would almost certainly find it an impossible task. Two of you might just manage it by putting the box down for frequent rests. Probably the best way, if you had no machine to help you, would be to push or drag it along. But if you put the same amount of earth into a wheelbarrow you would be able to lift and move it quite easily.

The wheelbarrow is a simple machine that makes use of two of our earliest inventions, the lever and the wheel. Of course, no one decided to invent the lever or the wheel, but one day someone – we do not know who, where or exactly when – tried them and found that they worked.

For thousands of years, people had nothing but their own muscles to help them till the soil, carry loads and lift or move objects. It is hard for us to imagine a world without machines of any kind, not even a wheel, but this was how our early ancestors lived. They used only the power of their arms and legs. As a result, they could **cultivate** only a little land very slowly and painfully, and perform only very simple carrying and lifting tasks.

The force or weight that you apply to a job of work is called the **effort**. A lever enables a certain amount of effort to do more work. Using

Without machines or beasts of burden we would have to rely on the power of our own muscles to carry, lift and move heavy loads. However, by using a lever, a load can be raised or drawn along more easily. Better still, we can use a wheelbarrow. This makes use of the lever, combined with another of the earliest inventions, the wheel. The effort needed for moving the load is now far less.

The ox-drawn plough (below) is a simple example of the use of a lever. The one shown here is an Egyptian model of 2000BC.

a wheelbarrow, you can lift more earth than you could possibly lift with your arms alone. Also, you can walk quite easily with a load that you could not manage without the wheelbarrow.

Our early ancestors spent a good deal of time growing food. It is possible to grow crops by simply scratching the soil with a stick and planting seeds in the scratches. However, things grow better if the soil is broken up thoroughly and turned over. By about 3000BC, picks made

of deer antlers were being used to dig the soil. The pick-head was driven into the ground and then levered out, turning over the soil as it came up. The invention of the plough was a great improvement on this, because it worked continuously instead of step by step. What was even better, it could be drawn by an ox, which did the hardest work. All the ploughman had to do was to steer the plough. A simple ox-drawn plough like this is still used in some parts of the world. It is one of the simplest examples of the use of a lever.

The wheel, too, turned 'step by step' tasks into continuous ones involving far less effort. The idea of the wheel probably came from an earlier idea of using tree trunks as rollers to

Tree trunks were once used as rollers to help in the transport of heavy loads. Even so, large teams of workers were still necessary in such an operation.

move heavy objects. This was slow, because the work had to stop frequently so that the position of the rollers could be changed. The first wheels were simply disks cut from tree trunks, which revolved on **axles** fixed to the underside of a cart or sledge.

Once wheels came into use, it became possible for humans to travel further to hunt or to trade, and to move their belongings more easily from one place to another. Soon, the clumsy, heavy, first wheels were improved upon. They were given iron rims to make them last longer. Then the solid wheel was replaced by a lighter

The Babylonians used an ox-drawn sled (right) in about 2000BC. The wheel was also in use, but a sled was better suited to travel over rough ground.

The wheeled Armenian ox-cart (left) of about 2000BC, with its light, A-shaped frame. This was easier to steer than the four-wheeled wagon of that time.

one, made up of spokes. This, in turn, meant that vehicles could travel faster, and horses, instead of oxen, began to be used to pull them along.

Almost as soon as it was invented, the wheel found another important use, other than transport. Before the potter's wheel was developed, pottery was crudely-shaped and uneven in thickness. Pots broke easily – often before the potter had finished making them – and often leaked. **Throwing** pots on a revolving wheel improved their quality, and made them last longer. They were also more pleasant to look at.

Therefore, by about 2000BC, our ancestors had taken some important steps forward. They had invented two machines, the lever and the wheel. In addition, they were able to adapt their ideas so that certain inventions could be used for other purposes. Now they no longer had to rely on their own strength alone. They had learned how to harness the power of animals.

The early civilizations

FOR THOUSANDS OF YEARS people did not live in communities. Each tribe or large family looked after itself, doing its own hunting and growing its own food. But when the plough had been invented and larger-scale farming became possible, people began to work more in groups. The best hunters would leave the best farmers to grow the crops, and then exchange meat for grain. People began to travel from one district to another to trade in goods. Gradually, the ancient world began to look more like today's. People lived together in villages and, later, cities, earning their living by buying and selling, or doing skilled work like pottery-making, spinning or weaving. **Civilization** had begun.

It is difficult to say exactly what 'civilization' means, but one way to describe it is to say that civilized people are those who have settled down to live permanently in one particular part of the world. If conditions are harsh and food is hard to come by, people move on in the hope of finding somewhere where life is easier. If they

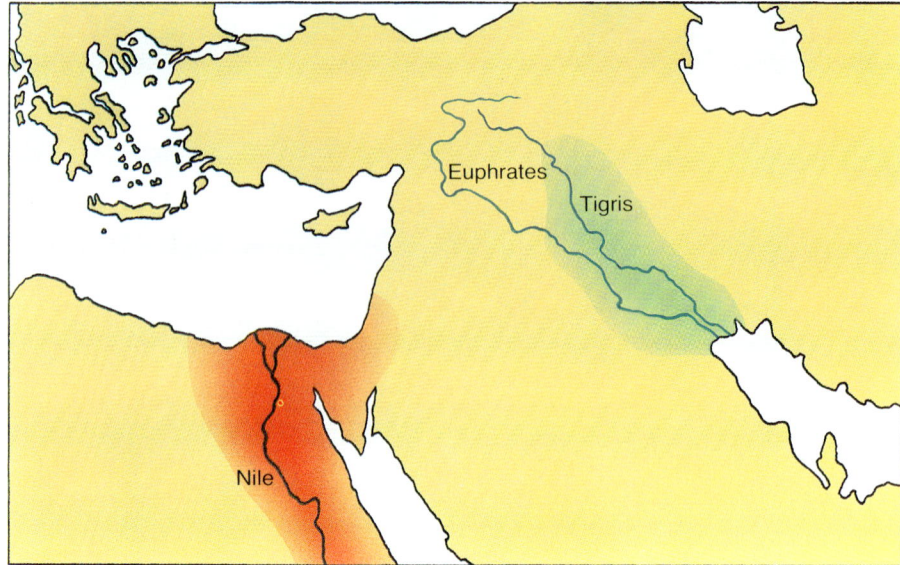

are successful, they are likely to settle there. This is what seems to have happened when the first civilizations grew up. This usually happened in areas where the land was **fertile**, and where great rivers provided another of the basic needs – water.

Some of the earliest civilizations were in the Middle East, where three great rivers, the Nile, the Tigris and the Euphrates, had made plains of rich, fertile river mud. This was not only good soil for farming, but the mud, shaped into bricks and dried in the hot sun, was an excellent building material. So the people of Ancient Egypt settled near the mouth of the Nile, and the people of Mesopotamia settled near the Tigris and Euphrates. They enjoyed an easier and more prosperous life than anyone had had before. They built great cities with beautifully decorated palaces. They enjoyed luxuries like making music, wearing jewellery and dancing, and they were very keen to try out new ideas.

All this wealth depended on prosperous and efficient farming, and the learned men of the early civilizations gave a great deal of attention to improving farming skills. One problem they tackled was the distribution of river water to

One of the earliest building materials was dried mud. It is still in use today, as can be seen in this patchwork of mud-brick buildings in Egypt. The material was close at hand in the form of river mud. The ancient Egyptians only had to shape the bricks, and leave them to dry in the hot sun.

The irrigation of fields, using ox power to raise and move water, was common in ancient times. It can still be seen in some parts of the world today. The lever and the wheel, as well as the ox, are used to great advantage. This system is continuous, and needs only one person to drive and feed the ox.

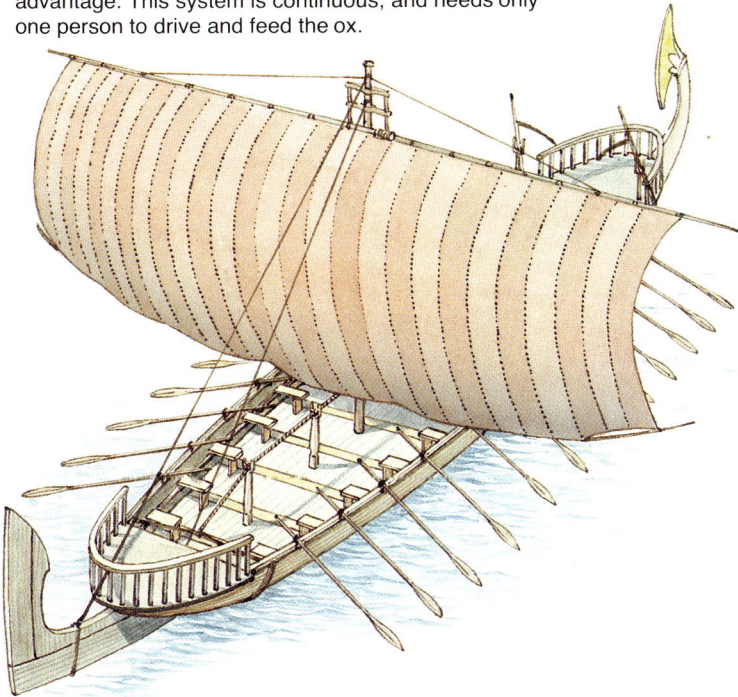

The Egyptians built wooden ships with sails as early as 3000BC. The Nile was as busy as a modern waterway, with trading galleys collecting linen, papyrus and other materials. These were exchanged for foreign goods such as timber, ivory and incense from other parts of the eastern Mediterranean.

irrigate their fields. This meant digging ditches and then lifting water from the river to fill them. The Ancient Egyptians found several ways of lifting the water.

One idea was to use a simple lever fixed to a wooden frame. At one end was a water-jar on a rope, and, at the other, a heavy rock. The weight of the rock lifted the full water-jar, which was then swung round and emptied over the ditch. Another idea was to use a system of **pulleys** to raise the jars. Later, the Egyptians invented a method of drawing water continuously, using ox-power. The ox operated a series of wooden wheels with pegs in their rims,

rather like gear-wheels. These were connected with another wheel which had jars strapped to its rim. The jars went down into the water and scooped it up. They then emptied it into the ditch at the top of the circle.

Irrigation was only one of the skills that the Egyptians brought to farming. Another was taking advantage of what they knew of astronomy. It was important to know when the Nile was going to flood, as it did every year in the summer. For this, a calendar was needed, and the Egyptians made one by studying the Sun and stars. They went on to develop other mathematical ideas, such as measuring areas by geometry, working out the points of the compass and calculating weights and measures. It was these skills that enabled the Egyptians to build their splendid cities and Pyramids.

Another important step forward that the Egyptians made was to use wind power for their boats. The first Egyptian boats were made of bundles of **papyrus** reeds tied together, but, later, planks of wood were used. There was a single square sail, with a large paddle at the stern for steering, and oars for use when the wind was slack. By about 2000BC the Egyptians had a large fleet of merchant ships travelling to other parts of the Eastern Mediterranean. Egypt, by now, grew enough grain to spare some for trading in exchange for timber and metal.

11

Athens and Rome

ABOUT 500 BC, the ideas of the civilizations of the Middle East began to spread towards southern Europe. There was a great deal of trade and travel between the Middle East and the states of Greece and Rome, and the people of these states adopted the new ideas and added to them.

The ancient Greeks and the Romans looked at the world around them in quite different ways. The Greeks enjoyed knowledge for its own sake and liked to understand the scientific laws on which the world is based. The Romans were more practical people, and they were more interested in putting knowledge to use.

One of the leading Greek scientists was Archimedes, who lived from 287 to 212 BC. As a young man, he went to Alexandria, in Egypt, to study science, and he spent the rest of his life studying and inventing. Archimedes was probably the world's first real scientist. He was not happy simply to invent something that worked. He wanted to know *why* it worked, and then to use the same principle to try out other ideas.

A pulley *(right)* is a simple device which the ancient Greeks used for lifting blocks of stone. The Archimedean screw *(below)* was used for lifting water. As the handle was turned, water was fed into the spiral screw. Since the screw kept moving, water was brought up to a trough or reservoir at the top of the machine.

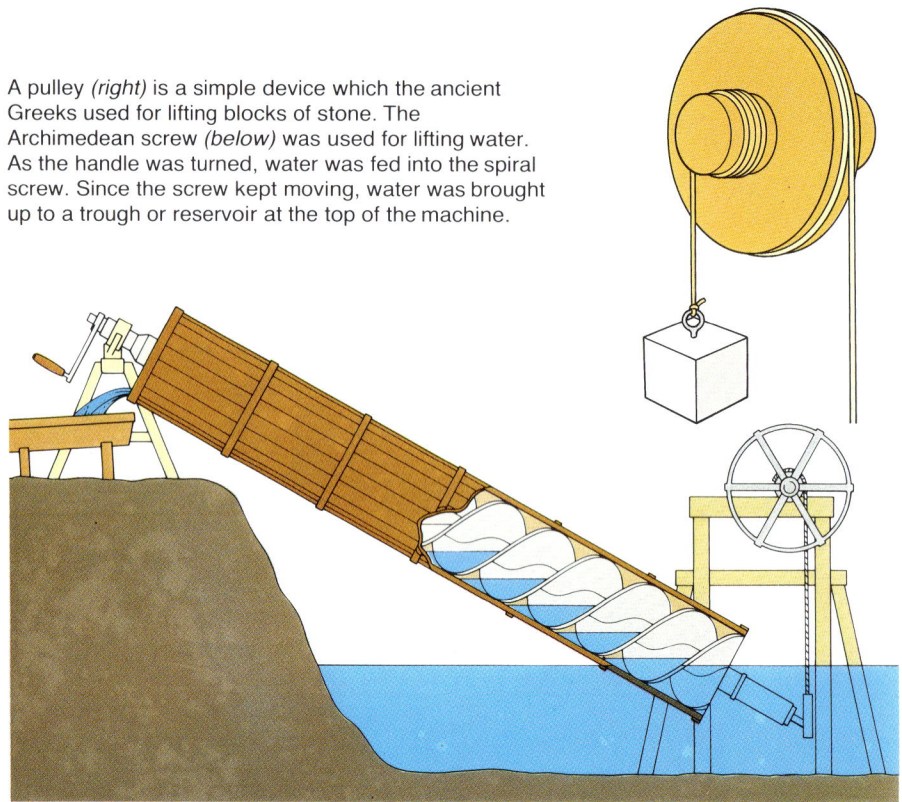

One of his inventions was a machine for irrigation which was called **Archimedes' screw**. Its great advantage was that it provided a continuous supply of water and could be operated by one man or one animal.

Although levers had been used for thousands of years, it was Archimedes who discovered how and why they work. He once said that if he had a lever long enough and somewhere to stand, he could move the earth. He became interested in the difference between the effort put into a task – of lifting weights, for example – and the amount of work done. The ratio of the work done to the effort put in is called the **mechanical advantage**.

The Greeks built many fine temples and other buildings in their cities. In order to do this they had to solve the problem of lifting large blocks of stone into place. They did this by using pulleys. A pulley is really a wheel with a grooved rim through which a rope can pass. Using one pulley may make a task seem easier, but in fact it takes just as much effort as lifting the load by

The Parthenon stands on the top of a hill called the Acropolis, overlooking Athens. This temple was built for the worship of the goddess Athena around 400 BC.

12

Water channel

The ancient Roman aqueducts were great feats of engineering. They were used to bring supplies of water from a distance to towns and cities where it was needed. Sometimes they built three-tier systems such as the one above. A similar aqueduct, the Pont du Gard, is still standing at Nimes in the south of France.

hand. There is no mechanical advantage. But two or more pulleys can be arranged so that the lengths of rope between them multiply the effort. By using compound pulley systems, the Greeks were able to do away with the ramps and slopes that had previously been used in building.

Meanwhile, scientific and technical ideas had moved westwards to Rome. From a small village in the centre of Italy, Rome had grown into a city which finally controlled an empire. By the first century AD, the Roman Empire covered most of southern and western Europe and part of the coast of North Africa.

The Romans learned their building skills from the Greeks, but they added many of their own. Rather than relying on water from wells or springs in the cities, they built **aqueducts**. These were stone pipes or channels to bring in water from a distant place. These aqueducts were carried across valleys on pillars, and this led the Romans to learn the art of building round arches. In order to do this they used a wooden frame to hold the stones in place until the mortar was dry. Arches were also used in buildings and bridges. In large buildings a series of arches was often used to form a vault.

To control the huge Roman empire, good communications were essential, and the Romans became expert road-builders. They invented a method of surveying the routes for their roads, which was not very different from the method used today. They used an instrument called a **groma**, a length of wood with a number of weighted strings hanging from it. Holding the groma at eye-level, the surveyor would line up the strings with marker posts driven into the ground at intervals of about 100 m.

Unfortunately, with the collapse of the Greek and Roman empires much of their knowledge was lost and had to be rediscovered over a thousand years later. If the Greek scientists and Roman engineers had continued to develop their skills, the early history of the world might have been very different.

The Romans were the first to build hard stone roads which were made to last. The foundations of the road consisted of layers of stones in mortar and above this a hard filling.

Moving mountains

(*right*) This sixteenth-century illustration shows an obelisk in Rome, being moved by the engineer Domenico Fontana, in 1586.

AFTER THE CIVILIZATIONS of ancient Greece and of Rome gradually came to an end because of war, there came a period of history in Europe in which few new discoveries or inventions were made. Some of the ideas developed by the Greeks and Romans were forgotten. One example of this is central heating. The Romans had invented a system of heating buildings with currents of warm air. However, this idea was forgotten for about 1500 years after the Roman civilization had ended.

However, the more simple machines, such as levers, **capstans** and pulley systems, were not forgotten. In the later Middle Ages, there was a great interest in Britain and parts of Europe in large building projects. These could not have been undertaken without the use of mechanical devices.

After the Normans conquered Britain they split up the land between them. The new owners of the land wanted to build castles to live in. At about the same time, the Christian religion expanded in western Europe. This meant that cathedrals and churches were needed where people could come to worship.

At about this time, a South American civilization, the Incas, was also creating large build-

Chartres Cathedral, France. Thousands of craftsmen and labourers were used to build this cathedral in the twelfth century. The heavy stone blocks and timbers had to be raised, using pulleys and capstans.

Evidence of the remarkable building skills of the Incas is still seen in the ruins of their mountain strongholds in Peru. The Incas ruled from 1476 to 1534 and in that short time their empire stretched some 3200 km.

ings and temples. Their technology differed in many respects from that of Europe, for instance they did not use the wheel. The Incan buildings were made of vast stone blocks cut with great skill. They were superb stonemasons.

The building projects in Europe brought together craftsmen of all kinds. These included stonecutters, carpenters, blacksmiths, glassmakers, metalworkers and stonemasons. A large work force of labourers was also needed. As the great stone pillars and walls were built, wooden **scaffolding** was erected so that stone blocks could be hoisted. The **windlass** and the capstan were essential for this heavy work. These were ancient Chinese inventions. They are similar machines, both based on the wheel. A force is applied to the rim of the wheel, turning the axle round which a rope is wound. In

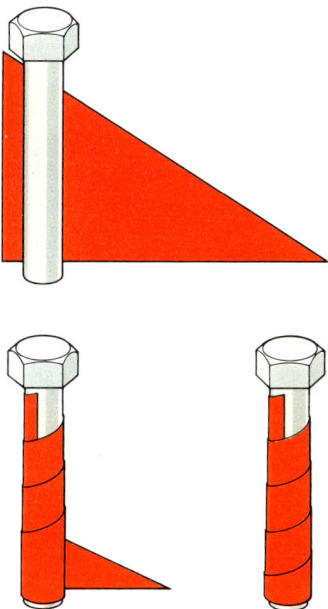

There are two main uses for the screw. One is for fixing two objects closely together, and the other is for raising a load. You can compare a screw with a spiral staircase. The effort required to climb the gradual slope of a staircase is less than that required to climb a vertical ladder. You are really climbing an inclined slope, as illustrated below.

building castles and cathedrals, builders used a kind of capstan which they called a 'great wheel' and which was big enough for one or two men to stand inside. Using capstans and pulleys, huge timbers for the roof trusses, and sheets of lead to cover the roof itself, could be hoisted into place.

The lifting of these heavy objects was a challenge to the builders. Their employers, the lords and the bishops, were asking them to perform very difficult tasks. In 1586 an engineer in Rome, Domenico Fontana, faced a great challenge. The Pope had decided that a great stone pillar, or **obelisk**, should be moved to a new site. The problem was that the obelisk weighed 312 tonnes, and stood 23 m high. Fontana prepared for the work carefully. He worked out the weight of the obelisk by cutting and weighing a model made of the same stone. He calculated that forty capstans could do the work, each worked by three or four horses. In all, about 800 men and 140 horses were necessary to complete the work.

First, a strong scaffold was built round the obelisk. Rush matting and a wooden jacket were added to protect the structure from damage during the move. Then wedges of wood and iron were driven under the base to raise it gradually and evenly. Rollers were placed underneath. With some capstans pulling, and others taking the strain so that the movement

was completely under control, the obelisk was slowly lowered on to its side. It was pulled on rollers to the new site where, again using the capstans, it was raised to the vertical, with wedges under the base. The final stage was to knock the wedges away and remove the scaffolding.

This was a great achievement, but Fontana's skill lay in his careful planning and organization rather than in any new ideas. He had calculated exactly where each capstan and team of horses should be positioned. He set up an elaborate signalling system so that each capstan could be started or stopped at any moment. During the operation, the movement of every capstan, the **tension** of every rope and the removal of every wedge was carefully timed. Fontana's relief when the job was finished must have been great. He admitted later, 'I had never combined so many different sources of power, nor seen anything similar'.

It is remarkable that so many of the sturdy and beautiful buildings in Europe were built between four and nine hundred years ago. Only human and horse power, and the simplest machines could be used to build them. However, the people who lived in those times were nearly at the limit of what they could do without the help of new sources of power. They had to wait to discover these before they could make any further great advances in **technology**.

Windmills and water-wheels

ONE OF THE FIRST problems that humans had to face when they began to grow **cereals** for food was that of grinding the grain into flour. At first this was done with a **pestle** and **mortar**. This was made up of a piece of stone held in the hand, and a stone bowl in which the grain was put. Grinding in this way was very slow work, and it took up time that could have been used for cultivating more land. Then it was found that grain could be ground between two flat, round stones, turning one against the other. This was an improvement on the pestle and mortar, but grinding grain was still a slow job.

By this time, sails were being used for boats, and someone had the idea of using windpower to turn a grindstone. Unlike the windmills we sometimes see today in the countryside, the first windmills had sails which went round horizontally, that is, parallel with the ground. Soon, these windmills were put to other uses as well as grinding corn. They were used for pumping river water for irrigation or pumping sea water into shallow pools to extract the salt.

Cutaway of a nineteenth-century windmill. This windmill had four sails which were connected to a drivewheel (A). The cap of the windmill was rotated to face into the wind by the fantail (B), or manually (C). The angle of the wooden shutters on the sails could also be adjusted, using a weight (D) on a rope. By means of gears and cogs, the vertical shaft (E) drove two upper millstones (F) against fixed stones. The grain was fed into the two cases through hoppers (G), to be ground into flour.

After about AD 1100, when the first windmills were built in Europe, there were many thousands at work. There were still some in use as recently as forty years ago. For about seven hundred years, most of Europe's flour was made by wind-power. However, windmills were not easy to use. The sails were easily damaged in high winds, and in Europe, where the wind blows from different directions at different times of the year, complicated arrangements were needed to turn the sails to catch the wind.

In northern Europe and many other parts of the world, however, there is no shortage of another source of natural energy – water. The Romans discovered how to use a water-wheel to turn grindstones by connecting them through a series of gears. The first water-wheels were of the '**undershot**' type where the wheel is made to turn by the pressure of water on the paddles at the bottom. However, in dry weather the water

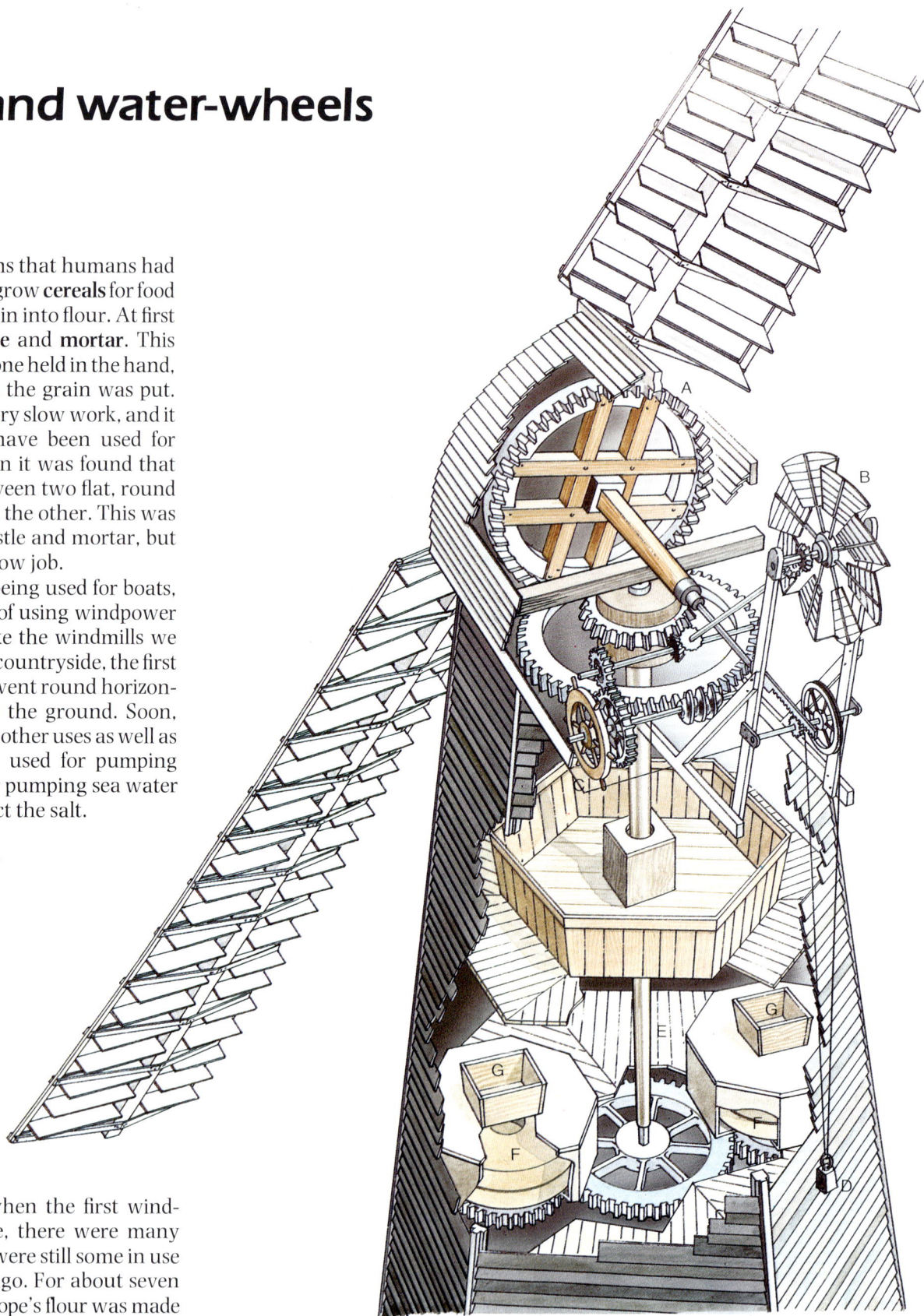

In this seventeenth-century smithy the power of a water-wheel is used for two purposes. It drives the bellows and also the hammer. As this is tripped up and down, the blacksmith forges the red-hot iron by altering its position on the anvil.

Two types of water-wheel. The overshot wheel *(left)* was fed with water from above, driving the wheel clockwise. The undershot wheel was fed with water from below, so that the wheel turned anti-clockwise.

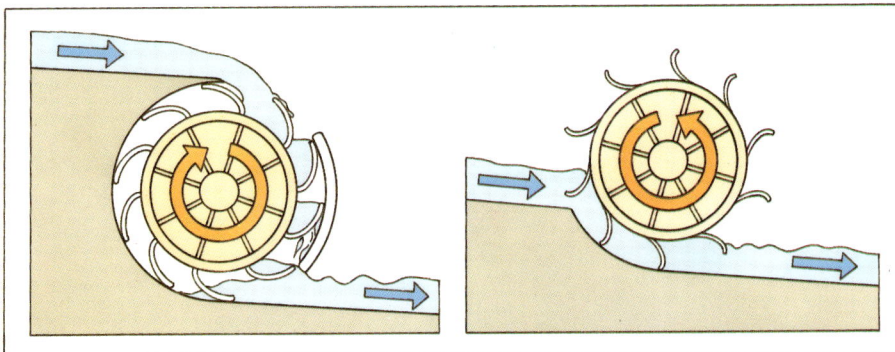

level might drop so that the wheel revolved only slowly or not at all. A reliable water-wheel needs a constant supply of water.

The answer was to store water by building a dam, and then to let the water reach the wheel in a controlled flow along a channel or through a pipe. With this type of wheel, the **'overshot'** type, the water fell on to the paddles from above, and its weight made the wheel revolve.

Using gears, a water-wheel could be used to do any kind of job that was continuous, such as grinding grain or pumping water. The next stage in the development of machinery was to work out a way of changing 'round and round' movement into 'up and down' movement. Once this was achieved, water-power could be used for many other kinds of work. The solution was the **cam**, a kind of wheel which is flat along part of its edge. It was mounted on a camshaft which

was connected to gears linked to the water-wheel. A beam was arranged so that it was in contact with the curved part of the cam. As the cam revolved, the beam would be raised, but when the flat part of the cam reached the top, cam and beam would lose contact, and the beam would drop.

The invention of the cam led to improvements in one important industry – the making of iron. Before this, the air that is vital to this process was supplied by hand-worked bellows. Only small amounts of poor quality iron could be made. However, bellows, operated by a beam worked through a camshaft from a water-wheel, enabled a continuous blast of air to be pumped into a furnace. Now, tonnes of iron could be made in a day, compared with only a few kilograms before. The principle of the cam and beam was soon used for hammering, another part of the ironmaking process. Up until this time hammering had been done by hand. An iron hammer was fixed on one end of a wooden beam, over an iron anvil. The beam was pivoted in the middle, with the cam at the other end. The cam lifted the hammer and then released it, when it came down to hit the newly-made iron on the anvil. Although the trip hammer, as it was called, was invented round about 1500, it remained in use long after steam had taken over from water as the source of energy for the ironmaking industry.

Spinning and weaving

CLOTHING is one of our basic needs. From the beginning of civilization, much time and skill have been spent in perfecting ways of making cloth, softening it, dyeing it and making it up into clothes. Early humans wore animal skins and furs, but by about 10000 years ago, people had learned how to spin thread. We know this because parts of the tools they used have been found. We do not know which was the first thread to be spun, but wool, cotton, flax and hemp were all used by our early ancestors.

Wool and cotton fibres both have to be spun into yarn before they can be used for making cloth. This involves drawing out and twisting the fibres. Until the 1760s this was done by hand on spinning wheels in the home.

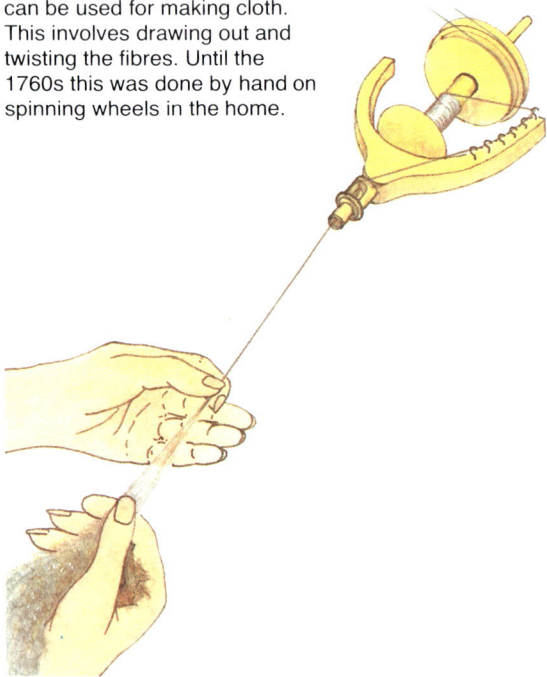

A thread is made up of millions of tiny **fibres**. The process of spinning straightens these fibres, twists them and then stretches them. You can try doing this for yourself with a small amount of cotton wool. If you live in the country, you could even use scraps of sheep's wool left behind on fences. Tease the material between your fingers, a little at a time, twisting it tightly and stretching it carefully as you go.

Thread made in this way is, of course, too uneven and too easily broken to be of any real use. The **spindle** was probably the first tool for spinning, and this was one of our earliest inventions. The spindle was rolled in the hand to twist the fibres and then allowed to hang

An early spinning wheel. The spinning wheel came to Europe from the Middle East in AD1200. The wheel was turned to draw out fibres of wool. These were wound into thread on a spindle. Early wheels were turned by hand, but by the sixteenth century a foot treadle was added. This enabled the spinner to have both hands free.

spinning by the thread to stretch and twist it further. The new length of thread was wound on to the spindle and work started on the next length.

This was a slow process, but it was speeded up when the spinning-wheel was invented. This was a frame in which the spindle lay on its side, connected by a loop of string to a large hand-turned wheel. The spinner turned the wheel with one hand and fed the fibres on to the spindle with the other. Later, a treadle was added so that the spinner could operate the wheel with one foot. This left both hands free to deal with the thread. Other small improvements were made, but until about two hundred years ago all cloth was made from thread or yarn spun in this way. Spinning was usually carried out by women and girls working in their own homes.

Once thread has been spun, it can be woven into cloth. One set of threads, called the **weft**, is passed over and under the threads of another set, the **warp**. Then each new line of weft is pushed against the previous one to make a close weave. The earliest weaving was probably done with a needle, as in darning. However, by the time of the early Middle East civilizations, the horizontal **loom** had been invented. Ancient Egyptian pictures show teams of women and girls working the looms. One turned a roller holding the newly made cloth while another separated the warp threads with a piece of wood. A third person passed the weft across the warp.

By about 1300, a greatly improved horizontal loom had arrived in Europe, probably from India. A framework of string or wire was used to separate the warp threads. This was moved up and down by a treadle, so that the weaver had both hands free. As it took so long to make, cloth was far more valuable than it is today. People of five hundred years ago would not dream of throwing away clothes just because they were tired of them, as we do now.

Then, about 250 years ago, there were a number of changes in spinning and weaving. Some were improvements to the machinery, and you can read about these in the next pages. Another was even more important, because it changed the daily lives of thousands of people. This was the introduction of water-wheels to provide the power for spinning and weaving. It meant that these jobs were no longer done by people working at home, but by large numbers of workers employed in factories. The spinners were the first to be affected, but by about 1830 there were thousands of hand-loom weavers out of work, while many more had had to go into the factories to earn a living.

The new factories made use of gears to bring energy from the water-wheels to the machines. The gears drove shafts which ran under the factory roof, and the shafts were connected to the machines by loops of strong material. However, water did not provide power for the spinning and weaving industries for long. Shortly after the first water-powered factories were built, the steam engine came into use. This was more reliable and factory owners soon changed over to this source of power.

When water power was introduced, machines could be used for cotton spinning and weaving. Quarry Bank Mill, in Cheshire, England is two hundred years old and has been brought back to life as a working museum by the National Trust.

The process of weaving is shown below. It is carried out on a loom. The warp yarns are fed from a beam through a harness. The weft yarn is fed to-and-fro across the warp yarns, as the harness lifts the warp yarns up and down. The result is woven cloth.

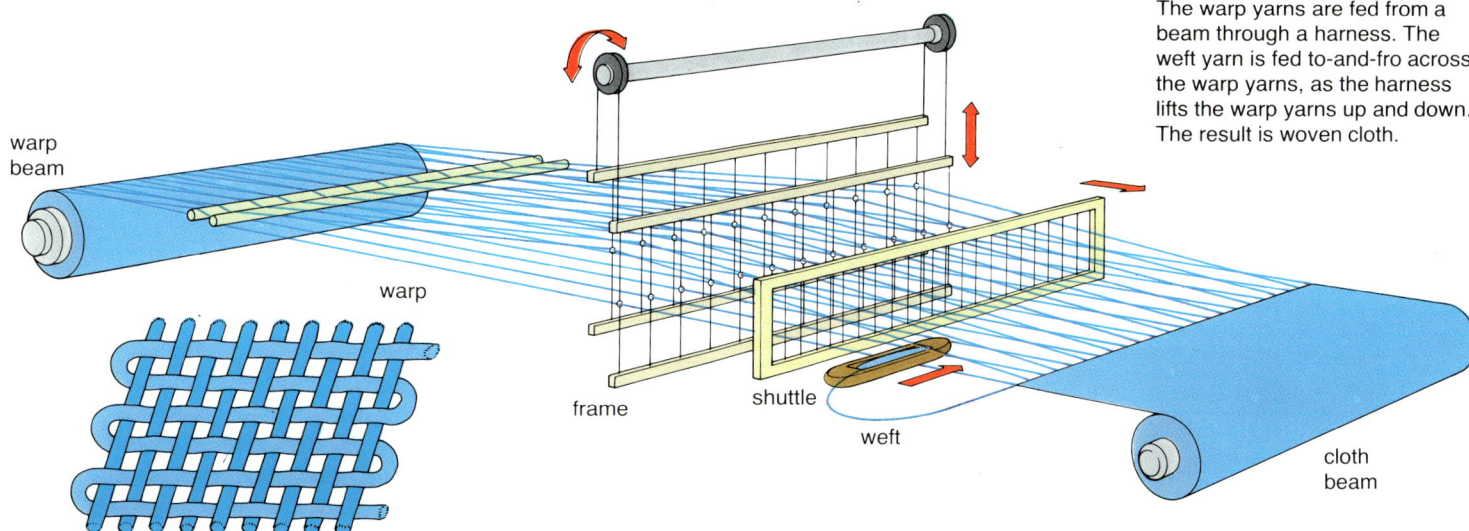

warp beam

warp

frame

shuttle

weft

cloth beam

The cloth machines

In less than one hundred years, spinning and weaving changed greatly. What had been carried out by hand in people's homes became machine operations in factories. This was because of a sudden burst of successful inventions. The first was the flying shuttle, produced by John Kay in 1733. The shuttle is the long **bobbin** which carries the weft thread from one side of the loom to the other. Before John Kay's invention, a shuttle had to be passed or thrown across by hand. The flying shuttle ran on wheels and could be sent from side to side across the loom by pushing a lever.

The flying shuttle was cheap and could be fitted to hand-looms, so it did not lead directly to factory weaving. However, it increased the speed of weaving, and soon there was a shortage of yarn. The next inventions were aimed at making thread and yarn more quickly. In 1765 James Hargreaves brought out his spinning jenny. Like the old-fashioned spinning wheel, this worked by turning a wheel by hand. However, the wheel was mounted on a frame containing eight **spindles** which could be wound at the same time. Later models could spin up to sixty threads at once.

Spinning jennies could be used at home, though they were expensive to buy. The next invention, however, was designed for factories.

A model *(above)* of the spinning jenny invented by James Hargreaves. This model could spin sixteen threads at the same time.

Flying shuttles *(left)*. The lower three are John Kay shuttles of the early eighteenth century. The three above are improved, later versions.

It was the water frame, the work of Richard Arkwright. While the thread produced by the spinning jenny was uneven and easily broken, the water frame made tough, even thread. However, it could not be worked by hand because it needed more power. The answer was to use water power, and factories were built alongside rivers in the north of England to provide power for the new machines.

About the same time, Samuel Crompton invented another spinning machine which he called a **mule**. This turned out to be particularly good for spinning fine thread. Crompton's own mule was worked by hand, but the larger models that followed needed waterpower to drive them.

Their working days were long, and they often faced a long walk to and from work. Many factory workers were children, some as young as four. They were employed because they could crawl under the machines to mend broken threads or pick up fluff, while the machines were still running. They worked for fifteen hours a day, sometimes longer, and were often so tired that they fell asleep at the factory. The foremen often beat them to wake them up. It was dangerous, miserable work for very poor

There was now more thread and yarn being spun than the weavers could use. It was, once again, the turn of weaving to be speeded up. A clergyman, Edmund Cartwright, was the first man to invent a weaving machine. Although he soon lost interest in it, other men took up his ideas and developed them. By the 1830s there were power-looms driven by water-wheels or steam engines. Now weaving had joined spinning as a factory occupation.

The new machinery made better, cheaper cloth and, in that way, changed people's lives for the better. However, for the people who worked in the factories it was a different story.

Crompton's spinning 'mule' *(above)*. The carriage rolled along a track twisting the thread. The yarn was wound on to the spindles as the carriage returned.

Child factory worker *(right)* in a cotton mill, Vermont, USA in 1910.

(below) The Joseph Harrison loom, 1851.

pay. It was many years before anything was done to improve conditions or prevent the employment of very young children.

What became of the inventors? John Kay was so upset by the protests of the weavers that his flying shuttle would put them out of work that he went to live in France. He died there soon afterwards, poor and unhappy. James Hargreaves opened a spinning mill in Nottingham, England. After losing a small fortune in trying to interest manufacturers in his loom, Edmund Cartwright turned to farming. Samuel Crompton set up a spinning business, but it failed and he died a poor man. Of this group of inventors, only Richard Arkwright became really wealthy. He went on to own a number of spinning mills, and when he died he left £2 500 000 which was a vast sum in those days. Together, these inventors made an industry which has given work to millions of people and cheap, attractive clothing to all of us.

The beam engine

THE SIGHT of a massive beam engine at work is always impressive. Fortunately some fine examples of these old engines have been preserved in working order. Most of those remaining were built to pump water. Beam engines were invented for that very purpose.

The first practical working steam engine was invented soon after the year 1700. The inventor was Thomas Newcomen, an ironmonger and blacksmith from Dartmouth in Devon, England. Very little is recorded of his experiments and failures. In 1712, Newcomen built his first successful, full-scale engine. A drawing made in 1719 shows all the details of this engine. It was huge. The engine house was about 10 m high, and poking through the wall of the engine house was half of the 8 m long oak beam. The beam rocked like a giant seesaw up near the roof.

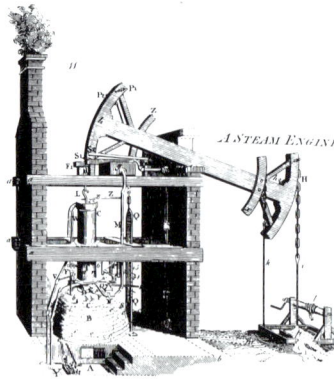

Newcomen's engine of 1712 (above). This splendid beam engine (below) has been restored in recent years, and is now in full working order. It produced 250 horsepower, and was used from 1876 to 1954 to pump water for two towns.

Why did these engines need this huge rocking-beam? The reason for the beam was to transfer power from the engine's single **cylinder** to the water pump. The pump itself was at the end of a long pump-rod down the mine shaft. Not surprisingly, this layout became known as a beam engine. Any other arrangement, without a beam, would have placed the engine over the mine shaft. This would have been neither practical nor safe.

How did the beam engine work? Inside the engine house, and under the end of the beam, was a long brass cylinder. Below the cylinder was a domed boiler, surrounded by brickwork. The boiler, with a coal fire beneath it, supplied the steam. Inside the brass cylinder was a **piston** which could slide up and down. The piston rod was connected to the beam by a chain. From the other end of the beam, another chain was fixed to rods. These reached 50 m down the mine shaft to work the water pump.

The engine always came to rest with the piston in the 'up' position. First, a steam **valve** was opened and steam filled the cylinder. Cold water was then sprayed into the cylinder. This caused the steam to **condense** into water and created a partial **vacuum**. The outside air pressure forced the piston down. This rocked the beam and pulled up the pump rods. About 45 litres of water were raised with each stroke of the pump. The piston then returned to the top of the cylinder, and the process was repeated. This type of engine is called an **atmospheric engine** because air pressure pushes down the piston.

Even on later Newcomen engines the steam valve was operated by a boy. A lazy but intelligent boy, called Humphry Potter, arranged a piece of cord so that the rocking beam worked the valve. This simple device became known as 'Potter's cord'.

In the 1760s, James Watt entered the scene. He was an instrument maker at Glasgow University. In 1764 he was given a working model of a Newcomen engine to repair. Watt realized that a great amount of heat was wasted, because the cylinder was always being heated up, and then cooled down. His brilliant idea was to have a separate **condenser** which would be connected to the cylinder. An air pump was also needed to suck air out of the condenser. This was worked from the beam.

persuaded Watt to adapt the **reciprocating**, (up and down), steam engine to produce **rotary**, (round and round), motion. This was needed for turning the new cotton-spinning machinery. Whilst Watt was still trying various ideas, James Pickard took out a **patent** which included the use of a crank. Watt therefore developed a system of gears to do the same job. In fact, it had the advantage of doubling the speed of the **flywheel**. A flywheel was necessary to smooth out the up-and-down motion of the engine.

Many other inventions were made by James Watt, and two were of special importance. In 1782, he patented the double-acting engine. Steam acted alternately on both sides of the piston, doubling the power and giving a smoother-working engine. This required a more rigid connection between the piston rod and the beam. In 1784, Watt devised his parallel link motion to guide the top of the piston rod in a straight line. He was very proud of this invention.

Beam engines, although huge and slow-moving, remained unchallenged for over one hundred years. Even when more compact vertical or horizontal steam engines were designed, the beam engine remained in use for pumping drinking water. Probably the last beam engine, working for its living, was at Addington, in Surrey, England. It ceased work in June 1975.

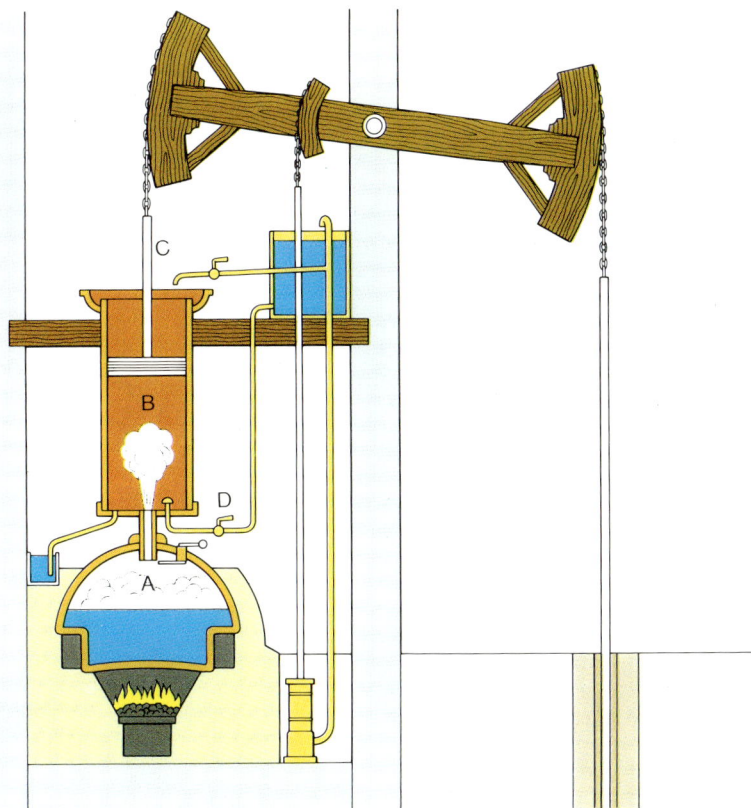

As a result of this invention, efficiency was greatly improved. A Newcomen engine would burn more than 1.5 kg of coal for each horse-power of work done. A James Watt engine, with separate condenser, could burn less than 0.5 kg of coal for the same amount of work.

James Watt went into partnership with Mathew Boulton in 1773. Boulton already had a factory in Birmingham, England, and a team of skilled workmen. Boulton could foresee the growing need for steam-power in factories. He

Newcomen's steam engine worked in this way. Steam produced by the boiler (A) was released into the cylinder (B), and the piston (C) raised. Cold water was then sprayed into the cylinder by valve (D) to condense the steam. This caused a partial vacuum and the outside air pressure forced the piston down again.

A Boulton and Watt double-acting steam engine, designed in 1784. The boiler (A) contained a constant amount of water. Steam entered the cylinder (B) through a pipe (C), setting the beam in motion. The cylinder was sealed at both ends. Two valves (D) opened and closed in turn. Opening the top valve helped to force the piston down. When this top valve was closed and the bottom valve opened, the piston was forced up again. The condenser (E) was below the cylinder. The pump rod (F) was connected to the beam (G) by a parallel linkage. This, in turn, was linked to a pump (H) which fed water from the condenser into a cistern (I).

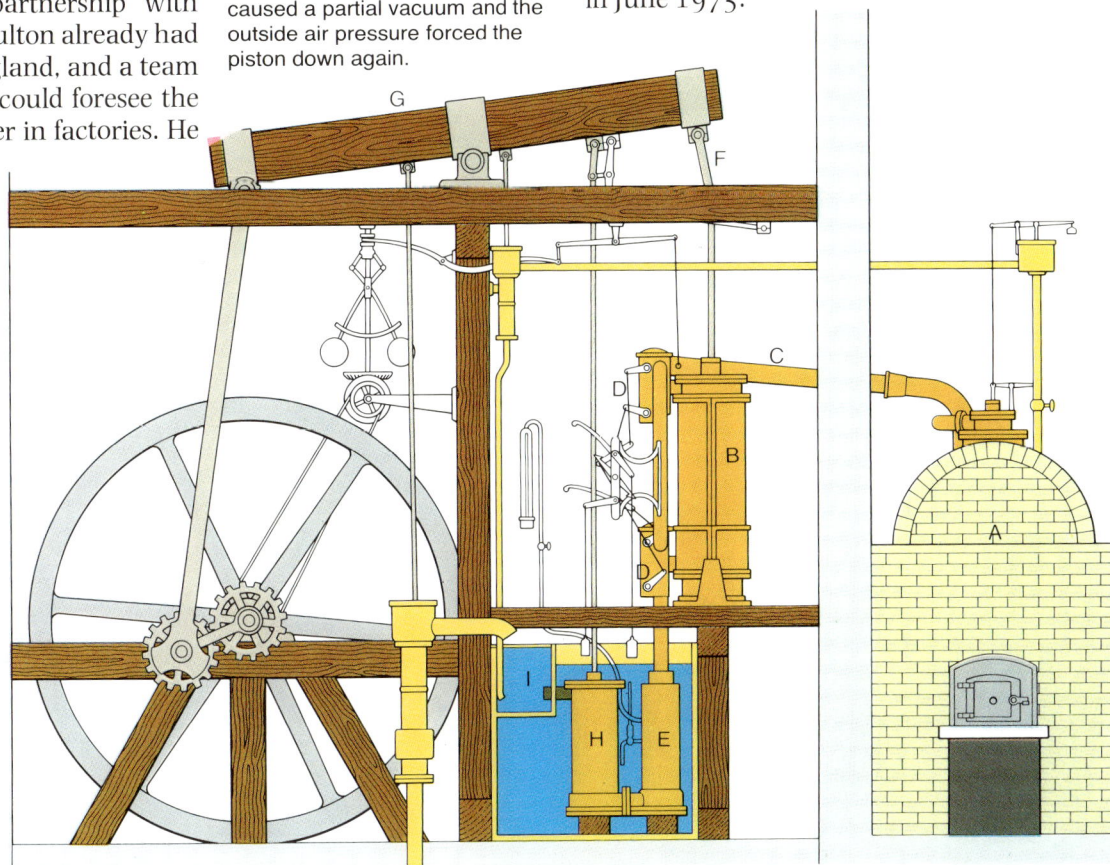

23

Pistons and cylinders

WHENEVER YOU PUMP up the tyre of a bicycle you are using a piston and cylinder. As you push the handle of the pump downwards you are forcing the piston down the cylinder. This action **compresses**, or squashes the air in the cylinder, and when the air pressure is high enough it passes through the valve into the inner tube of the tyre.

A beam engine and a motor-cycle do not appear to have much in common, but both can be driven by a single cylinder and piston. The first practical steam engine was built about 270 years ago. However, the history of a piston moving inside a cylinder goes back about two thousand years when a crude device was used to pump water.

The German scientist Otto von Guericke, who was the mayor of the city of Magdeburg, carried out a famous experiment in the 1650s. He had made a metal sphere in two separate halves, or **hemispheres**, with only an airtight seal between them. When the air was pumped out of the sphere, sixteen horses were not strong enough to pull the two hemispheres apart. He repeated the experiment with a piston and cylinder, and this time sixteen strong men, hauling on a rope fixed to the piston, could not overcome the force of the vacuum.

Around 1680 Christiaan Huygens, a Dutch astronomer, and his French assistant Denis Papin built a gunpowder engine, which was like a cannon with a piston instead of a cannon ball. Although this experiment was a failure, we can think of it as one of the first attempts at making an **internal combustion** engine.

Denis Papin, who also invented the pressure cooker, carried on with his own experiments. He boiled water in a brass cylinder, fitted with a piston 6 cm in diameter. He then cooled it

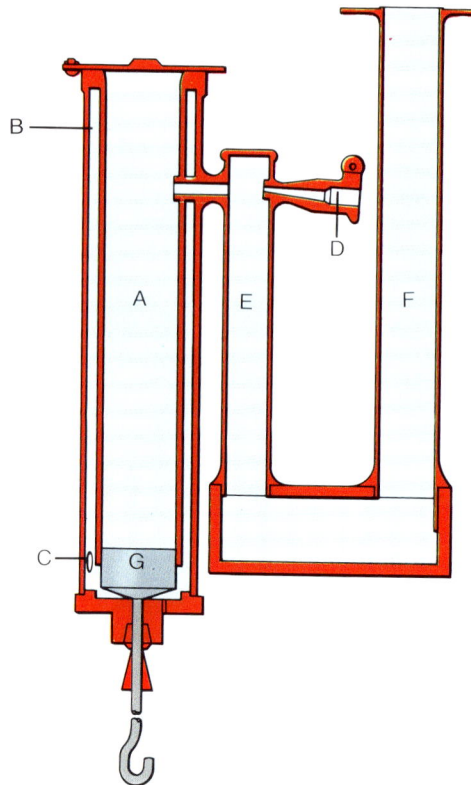

(left) Watt's model of a steam engine with a separate condenser. Steam enters the cylinder jacket (B) through a valve (C). Air from the cylinder (A) is forced out through a valve (D) as the cylinder fills with steam. When (A) was filled with steam, a piston in (F) was raised, sucking steam into (E) and (F). At the same time (E) and (F) were submerged in cold water, and the steam condensed. A partial vacuum was formed and up went the piston (G).

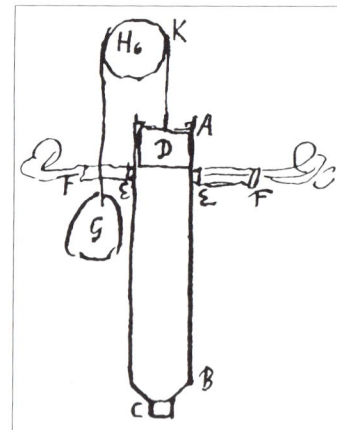

A sketch (above) by Christiaan Huygens, explaining his gunpowder engine of 1673. Gunpowder was exploded at (C) forcing the piston (D) up. Exhaust gases then escaped through valves (E) and (F). As the piston fell back down the cylinder, a weight (G) connected by a rope (K) over a pulley (H) could then be raised.

Von Guericke's experiment of 1672. This proved that the power of many horses was not enough to pull two hemispheres apart. They could not overcome the great force of the vacuum holding the two hemispheres together.

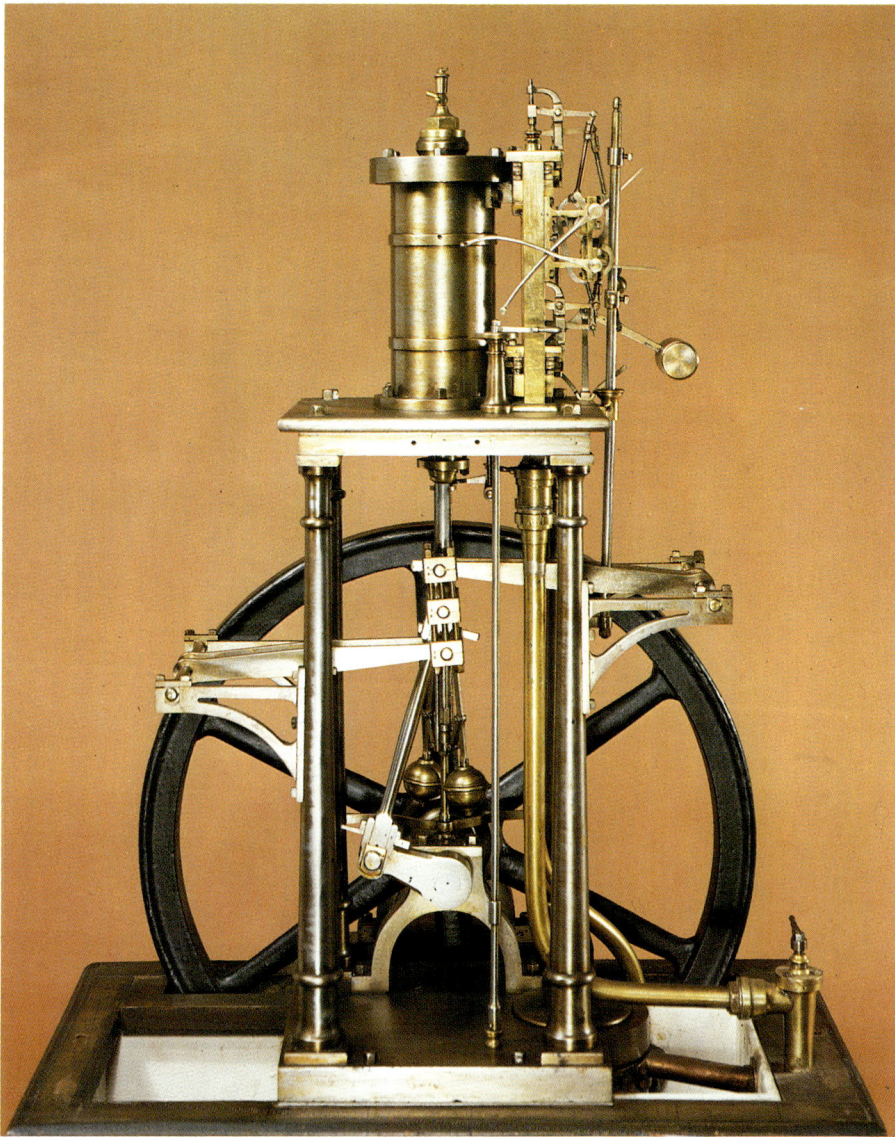

A model of an inverted single-cylinder engine used for pit winding gear, built according to a design by James Watt in 1812.

James Watt did not, as most people believe, invent the steam engine, but he made a great many important improvements. He, too, had problems with steam leaking past the piston. In those days it was said that a piston was a good fit, if a shilling coin would not fit between piston and cylinder. Nearly everything was tried as a seal, but hemp still proved the best.

The problem of piston seals increased as engineers began to use greater steam pressures. John Wilkinson of Wrexham, in Wales, devised a new machine for boring cannon barrels. A hard cutting tool was driven round and round inside the cylinder on the end of a strong bar. This gradually cut away the metal and made a cylinder which was nearer to perfection.

Steam engines became larger, with steam pushing the piston upwards and downwards. By the end of the eighteenth century there were steam engines at work in mines, mills, iron works and breweries. The Cornish engineer, Richard Trevithick, appeared on the scene at about the time James Watt was retiring in 1800. Whereas Watt believed in low-pressure engines, Trevithick favoured high-pressure engines. His engines were therefore smaller, more powerful and more efficient. This opened up the possibility of using steam engines to power vehicles and boats.

Steam appeared to have no rivals as a source of power in the first half of the nineteenth century. As the engines themselves became more powerful and efficient, so too did the factory **lathes** and drilling machines. They were able to manufacture pistons and cylinders which fitted each other precisely. We call this **precision engineering**. This helped the development of the internal combustion engine, which depends upon pistons fitting inside cylinders with the greatest possible precision.

In 1876 a German engineer, Nikolaus Otto, built the first successful internal combustion engine. It had a single cylinder and piston. Its fuel was burnt inside the cylinder, rather than outside as in the case of the steam engine.

down, so that the steam condensed, forming a partial vacuum under the piston. The pressure of the atmosphere on the outside of the piston forced the piston down the cylinder. Using a system of cord and pulley, the piston was able to lift a weight of 28 kg in the process. Although Papin's model was the first atmospheric steam engine, it was many years before anyone succeeded in building a large engine capable of doing useful work.

It was left to Thomas Newcomen to build the first full-sized working steam engine. He was a blacksmith, and his partner, John Calley, was a plumber and tinsmith. Together they made a brass cylinder with an internal diameter of about 48 cm. The inside of the cylinder had to be carefully shaped using hand tools. Even so there were leaks of air and steam past the piston. Moistened **hemp**, a material used for making rope, was packed tightly round the piston, and this acted as a seal.

Hemp was at first used as a means of sealing the gap between a piston and cylinder (left). The modern way of doing this is to use piston rings (right). This requires precision engineering.

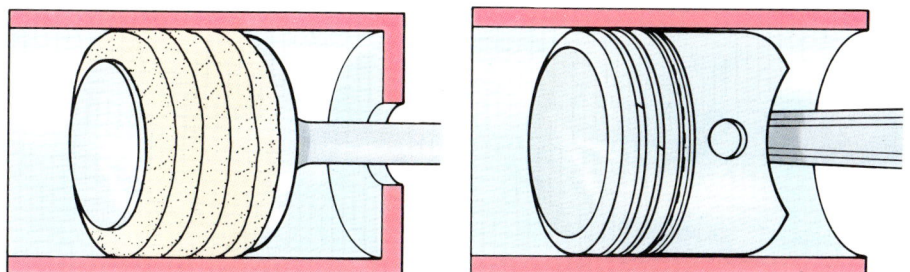

The first steam locomotives

The first steam locomotives, similar to this design, were built in 1803 by Trevithick for use at the Coalbrookdale Ironworks in Shropshire, England. He was able to prove that a steam locomotive could pull much more than a horse could pull.

ANY HISTORY of steam locomotives must include a discussion of the track they run on. But did you know that railway track was in use a long time before the first steam locomotive was built? A book published in 1556 describes medieval mining. A drawing in this book shows a wagon running on a trackway of planks. A big disadvantage of tracks like this is that the wheels run off the edge of the planks. The way to overcome this problem is to fit a **flange** (a raised edge) either to the track or to the wheels. A flange on the track needs to be fitted along the whole length of both tracks. A better and cheaper way is to fit a flange to the inside face of each wheel. This type of flanged wheel is used by all modern wheeled railways.

An account written in 1676 records that a horse was able to pull a load of 2.25 tonnes of coal in wagons on a wooden track. But the horse could pull only one tonne on an ordinary road. Iron tracks, or rails were even better. The first iron rails were no more than cast iron plates laid on top of wooden tracks. The self-supporting iron rail came later. Even today the railwayman who lays rails is still called a plate-layer.

Richard Trevithick built the first steam locomotive to run on iron rails. A South Wales ironmaster called Samuel Homfray bet a friend that a steam locomotive could be made to haul a ten tonne load over the ten mile Pen-y-Derren tramway. Trevithick's locomotive did this easily, but the weight of the locomotive broke the cast-iron tramway in several places. The engine was soon dismounted and used to drive a hammer in the ironworks as Trevithick had intended.

Trevithick's second locomotive appears not

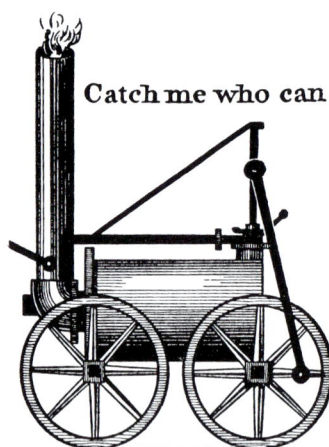

Catch me who can

Trevithick's London locomotive, *Catch-me-who-can*, was built in 1808. It was said to be capable of a speed of nearly 20 kph.

Before the invention of the flanged wheel *(below)*, wagons were kept on the track of planks by means of a raised edge *(left)*.

to have been used. In 1808 he built his third. It was called '*Catch-me-who-can*' and ran on a circular track near the site of the present-day Euston station in London. For a 'shilling-a-go' passengers could ride in open wagons. The train attracted much attention but made little money.

In 1812 there came a turning point. Until this date all the steam locomotives built had been short-lived experiments. From now on there was to be some commercial success. Because of the Napoleonic wars the cost of feeding horses had become very expensive. There were a number of colliery railways that had existed for many years and they used horses for hauling coal trucks. However, there was now the possibility of replacing many horses with a small number of steam locomotives.

John Blenkinsop was the manager of the Middleton coalmine near Leeds, England. He placed an order for two steam locomotives of his own design. The existing coalmine railway was laid with special rails. They were of cast-iron and had **rack** teeth cast into the outside of one rail. Four engines of sound design were eventually built. Each had twin cylinders which drove a rack-wheel. The teeth of the rack meshed with the teeth cast into the rail. Each engine did the work of sixteen horses. It was soon found that a rack railway was only really necessary on mountain railways.

The Wylam coalmine on Tyneside decided to

The original development model *(left)* of Timothy Hackworth's locomotive *Sans pareil*, built in 1828. In the following year the Liverpool and Manchester Railway held the Rainhill Trials, at which *Sans pareil* was beaten by George Stephenson's *Rocket*.

Original development model of George Stephenson's locomotive No.1 *Locomotion*, built in 1825.

A working replica of Stephenson's *Rocket*. The competing locomotives at the Rainhill Trials in 1829 had to complete a course equal to 56km, take on more fuel and water, and then complete a further 56km. Each locomotive had to tow a load three times its own weight. This locomotive was the true prototype of the steam locomotive family that spread throughout the world.

build its own locomotives. William Hedley studied the Middleton engines and improved on them. Apart from doing away with the rack he designed a more efficient boiler working at twice the pressure of Trevithick's engine. However, he had trouble with the weight of the locomotive breaking the rails. He therefore increased the number of axles to spread the load. Three similar engines were built: *Puffing Billy* (now in the Science Museum, London), *Wylam Dilly* (now in the Edinburgh Museum) and *Lady Mary*. These locomotives were at work until the colliery closed in 1862.

An interesting failure of this period was William Branton's locomotive. This had a single cylinder which drove two legs complete with 'feet'. Sadly the engine blew up on test, killing its crew.

Wylam village was, in 1781, the birthplace of George Stephenson. His father was a fireman at Wylam coalmine. By 1812 George was in charge of all the machinery belonging to the Grand Allies collieries. The following year he was asked to build a steam locomotive for the Killingworth colliery railway. His first locomotive was called the *Blucher* and ran in July 1814. During the next twelve years he built no fewer than sixteen locomotives.

On his second locomotive he made an important improvement in design. Up to this point nearly every locomotive used a train of gears between the crank and the driven wheels. These were both noisy and inefficient. George

Stephenson and a certain Mr Dodd decided to couple the connecting rods directly to the driven wheels. This was done using a crankpin set into the wheel. To understand this, just take a look at the *Rocket* in the illustration.

In 1821 a British Act of Parliament authorized a public railway between Stockton and Darlington. It was to carry passengers as well as goods and would use steam locomotives. The line was opened on 27th September 1825 and the first train was hauled by the locomotive *Locomotion*. *Locomotion* developed about 10 horse power and could pull a load of 60 tonnes at 8 kph. The Stockton and Darlington railway became the first public railway to use steam power.

Railways of the world

RAILWAYS were a British invention, but other countries quickly took up the idea. One of the first was the United States. In 1830, only five years after the opening of the Stockton and Darlington Railway, the first, successful, American steam locomotive, *The Best Friend of Charleston*, made its first run. By 1833, the South Carolina Railroad between Charleston and Hamburg, a distance of 216 km, was the longest in the world. Soon, there was a network of lines linking the important towns of the East Coast states, especially in the coal-mining areas of Kentucky and West Virginia.

It became the dream of American railway-builders to build a line right across the country, linking the Atlantic and Pacific. In 1864 work began. The Central Pacific company worked east from San Francisco and the Union Pacific started out from Omaha, Nebraska, the furthest point west that the railways had reached. Be-tween them lay 3000 km of prairie, desert and mountains. Most of the building materials had to be carried huge distances. It was bitterly cold in winter and uncomfortably hot in summer. The railway-building gangs were attacked by buffalo, Indians and criminals. Despite all this, the two gangs met in 1869, at Promontory Point in Utah. Here, the last spike – a golden one – was driven into place, and workmen posed for photographs before sitting down to a celebra-tion meal. Other transcontinental lines were later built across America, but it was the Omaha to San Francisco line that first opened up the prairie states.

Operating railways in America was far more difficult than in Britain. The **gradients** were steeper and the curves of the track tighter. The weather was more severe. The transcontinen-tal tracks were not fenced and animals often strayed on to them. These conditions led Ameri-

Driving in the 'Golden Spike', at Promontory Point, Utah, on 10th May 1869. This early photograph records the event. The Central Pacific locomotive, (left), from California, meets the Union Pacific locomotive from Omaha.

An early American locomotive *(left)* in mountain country. Note the cowcatcher, the searchlight and the large smokestack designed to prevent sparks from setting fire to forests and prairie.

The Trans-Siberian railway *(below)* stretches across the desolate wastes of Russia. This railway was built between 1891 and 1904, linking Leningrad and Moscow with Vladivostok on the Pacific coast.

country to be opened up was Russia. It was decided to build a railway from Moscow across Siberia to Vladivostok on Russia's Pacific coast. This was an even more difficult task than those faced by the American and Canadian railway-builders. Along part of the route the land is frozen solid during the winter, but turns to swamp in the summer. On the borders of Europe and Asia there are the Ural Mountains to be crossed, and there are more mountains further east. It took ten years to build the Trans-Siberian Railway. Even so, for several years there was a gap where the route crossed Lake Baikal, close to Russia's southern border with

can engineers to design locomotives that looked quite different from those of Britain. They were heavier and more powerful. Most of them used wood for fuel, and had wide funnels to catch the sparks. There was a large headlamp in front of the funnel to light up any obstacles on the track, and a 'cowcatcher' to sweep them away. Engines often had a four-wheeled **bogie**, pivoting on its own, in front of the driving wheels. This was designed to smooth out the ride and help the locomotives around sharp curves. This idea was later also used for passenger carriages and large goods wagons.

Canada, also, wanted to open up the thousands of kilometres of wild and almost empty country between its Atlantic and Pacific coasts. In 1881 work started on the Canadian Pacific Railway. The line had to be driven through the Rocky Mountains in the west, across the wide open prairies, over solid rock and across swamps. Some engineers had said that the task was impossible. In 1885, however, people were able, for the first time, to travel by train from Vancouver in British Columbia to Montreal. Before railways were developed, this journey took five months. Now, it could be done in five days.

Another country with a vast area of wild

The Paris to Lyons super-express *(right)* can reach a speed of 240kph. To enable the express to travel at high speeds around curves the track is banked as shown here.

The Bluebell railway *(below)* in Sussex, England. The locomotive was built in 1872, and is still running as a tourist attraction.

Mongolia. In summer, passengers were ferried across the lake by boat, but in winter the train simply took to the ice. Later, a line was built round the southern shore of the lake.

The great transcontinental railways opened up vast countries for settlers and industry. Engineers had to find solutions to many problems, and the discoveries they made were useful in all sorts of construction work. Some of their ideas are still used in road-building and engineering today.

29

The horseless carriage

IT IS DIFFICULT for us to imagine a time when people rarely travelled more than a short distance from their homes. When the horse was the only means of transport overland, travel was slow and difficult. It was also uncomfortable and expensive.

Once the steam engine had been invented, many engineers tried to make steam-powered vehicles for the road. In 1769 a Frenchman, Nicolas Cugnot, built a three-wheeled 'steam wagon' which was not designed to carry passengers, but to pull heavy guns. Cugnot's first model was destroyed when it crashed into a wall, but two years later he built another. It was not a success, probably because its top speed was only about 3 kph.

By 1830, a number of successful steam road vehicles had been built, and there was a steam-carriage service in Britain between Bath and London. But the 190 km journey took over nine hours, along rough, potholed and rutted roads. Within a few years, the Great Western Railway had been built in Britain, and the train journey took less than half the time. With the coming of the railways, most people lost interest in steam-powered passenger travel on the roads. However, in the United States, where the railway network was built up more slowly, experiments continued. Richard Dudgeon's steam car, built in 1857, was one of these. One American company, Stanley, even went on making steam cars until the 1920s.

Cugnot's steam wagon consisted of a wooden chassis with three wheels. A boiler at the front fed two cylinders which drove the single front wheel. Its major drawback was that it was hard to steer and it ran out of steam in 12–15 minutes.

A Dion-Bouton steam motor that won the Paris-Rouen race in France in 1894.

Things were different with goods traffic. Until about sixty years ago, steam wagons and **traction engines** were quite common sights on the road. Steam wagons had boilers and funnels in front of the open cab, like railway locomotives, and a truck body behind. Traction engines were self-contained locomotives which pulled numbers of trucks.

If a machine was to be used with the same ease, convenience and speed as a horse and carriage, it needed to be lighter than a steam vehicle. It also needed to use lighter and more convenient fuel. The answer began to take shape in Europe in the 1860s, when many inventors were trying out ideas for engines driven by gas or petrol. No single person can be given the credit for inventing the **internal combustion engine**, but in 1876 Nikolaus Otto built the first successful engine to use the 'four-stroke' principle.

Just as there was a gap between the invention of the steam engine and the building of a steam locomotive, several years passed before Otto's engine was fitted into a car. There were several problems to be solved. How should a car be steered? How could it be made to slow down or stop? How should the engine be started? What should a car look like? Another German engineer, Gottlieb Daimler, joined Otto about this

time. He had a simple answer to the last question. Take a horse carriage, he said, cut off the shafts, and fit an engine underneath. The first Daimler car, made in 1885, looked exactly like its name – a horseless carriage. In fact, it made good sense to use the carriage design, because, outside towns, the roads were still only cart-tracks and the car body had to be kept well clear of the ground.

In the same year as Daimler, another German, Karl Benz, also produced his first car. This was lighter than Daimler's, and could carry only the driver and one passenger, compared with the four people who could travel in Daimler's car. The Benz car was a three-wheeler, which was very slow and had difficulty in climbing slopes. The two men treated their inventions quite differently. Almost at once Benz

A Foden steam lorry (above) with the boiler visible underneath the cab.

A steam traction engine (right).

Gottlieb Daimler riding in his petrol motor in 1886.

The four strokes of Otto's internal combustion engine, shown from left to right. At the first stroke a fuel/air mixture is fed into the cylinder. At the second stroke the mixture is compressed. At the third stroke the mixture is ignited and at the fourth stroke the exhaust gases are forced out of the cylinder

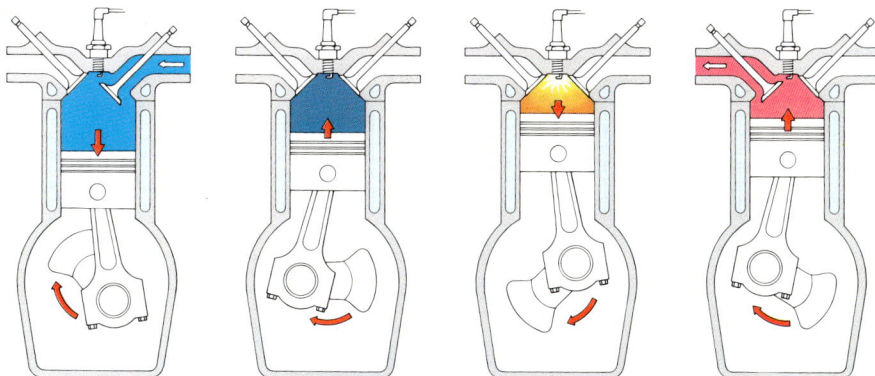

began making large numbers of cars, keeping to the same design for over fifteen years. Daimler went on making improvements to his engine, and, instead of building cars himself, he sold the engines to a French company, Panhard and Levassor, who fitted them into their own car bodies.

Benz's car was simple and reliable, an important point when there were no garages and few trained mechanics. Daimler's was faster, more comfortable, but more liable to break down. But between them they were the true founders of the automobile industry.

How a modern car works

In a modern car we can find examples of a large number of the different machines which have been invented. Some, such as the wheel and the lever, are very old and others more recent. For example, the internal combustion engine is a fairly recent invention. A car is really a kit made up of many different machines. The engine provides the power. The **transmission** carries the power through gears to the driving wheels. The steering system enables the driver to control the direction in which the car travels. The braking system reduces the car's speed when necessary. Many other devices help in the safe and comfortable driving of a car. These range from the small motors that drive the

Most vehicles today use a steering system similar to this one, known as a rack and pinion *(left)*. The pinion is rotated by the steering column, so moving the rack. The rack then moves the wheels, steering the car to the left or right.

heater fan and the windscreen wipers to the **electromagnet** that operates the horn.

The kind of internal combustion engine invented by Nikolaus Otto is still used in most cars today. In this engine, a mixture of petrol and air burns in the cylinder, and this forces the piston downwards. This force provides the power to turn the driving wheels, but several things happen to it on its way from the engine to the wheels. Each piston is connected by a rod to the **crankshaft**. Because of this, each downward movement of the piston makes the crankshaft turn through part of a **revolution**. This changes the up-and-down motion of the pistons to the circular motion that is needed to drive the wheels.

The crankshaft revolves at high speed, and this must be converted to the lower speeds that

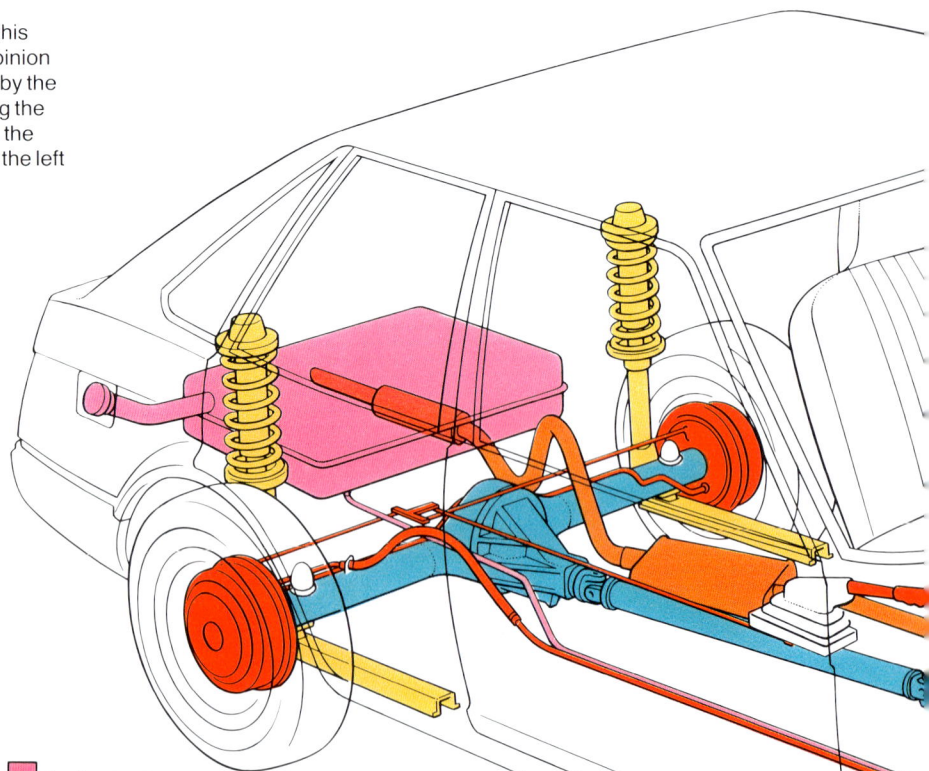

are needed to turn the driving-wheels. This is done by the gearbox, which contains different gears. There are usually four forward gears and one reverse, each suited to the different kinds of work the car has to do. First, or bottom, gear converts the drive of the engine into a very powerful force for use in moving off from a standstill, or for climbing steep hills. Once the car is on the move, less force is needed and the driver changes up into second gear. Third gear is normally used if the car is travelling at moderate speed in traffic, and sometimes for passing. The fourth, or top, gear in most cars is used for **cruising** on the open road. In cars with manual gearboxes the driver makes the gear

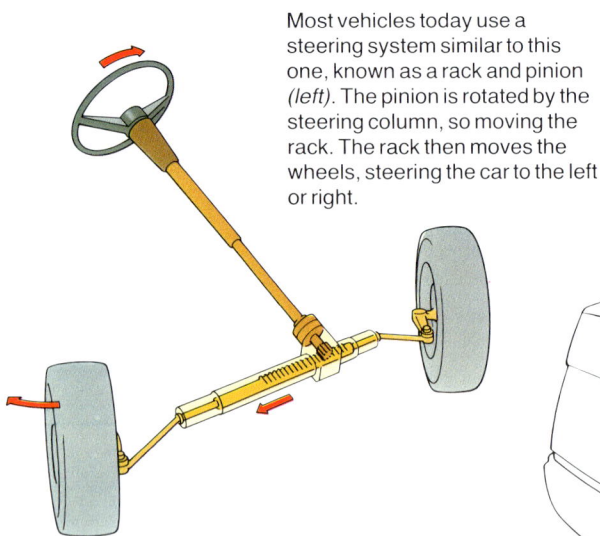

fuel system

braking system

suspension system

steering system

cooling system

electrical system

engine

exhaust system

transmission system

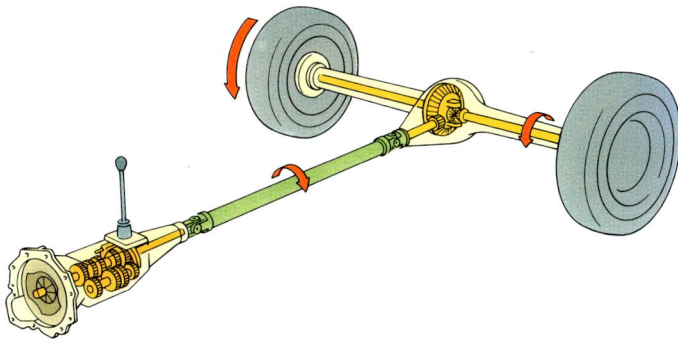

A transmission system in a rear-wheel drive vehicle includes the gearbox, propeller shaft, differential and half-shafts, which make up the rear axle. The differential has three purposes. Firstly it gears the speed of the spinning propeller shaft down to suit the road wheels; secondly it converts the drive through 90° to turn the wheels; thirdly it allows the inside wheel to revolve slower than the outside when the vehicle goes around a corner.

changes, but automatic gearboxes adjust themselves to suit the speed and driving conditions.

Power leaves the gearbox along the output shaft and travels down the car from front to back. In a car with rear-wheel drive, the output shaft is connected to a **propeller shaft** which runs to a further set of gears called the **differential**. These gears have two jobs to do. First, they convert the front-to-back direction of the drive to a sideways one. Second, they allow each of the driving wheels to revolve independently on

A hydraulic brake system *(right)*. When the brake pedal is pressed hydraulic fluid is forced through pipelines to the slave cylinders, which act on the brake. The pressure that the slave cylinders exert is considerably greater than the pressure of the foot on the brake pedal.

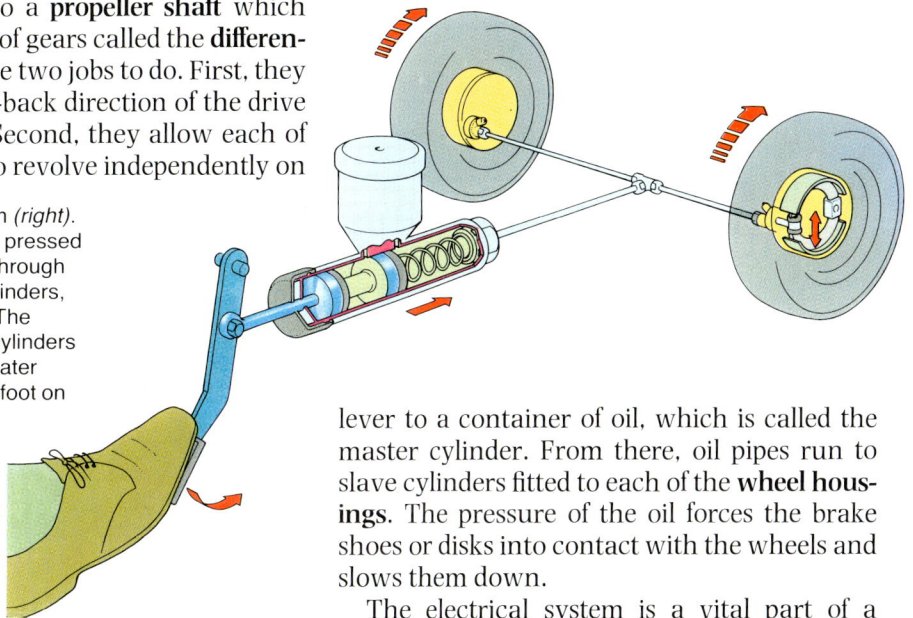

their own **half-shafts**. This is necessary because, in turning a corner, the wheel on the outside of the curve has farther to travel than the one on the inside. Some cars have front-wheel drive.

All cars have their steering systems connected to the front wheels. Quite a small turn of the steering wheel causes a large change of direction. Gears inside the steering system increase the amount of work done by the driver's hands. These gears also convert the circular movement of the steering wheel into the to-and-fro movement needed to turn the front wheels.

Braking systems make use of **hydraulic**, or fluid, power. When the driver presses a foot on the brake pedal, the force used is carried by a

lever to a container of oil, which is called the master cylinder. From there, oil pipes run to slave cylinders fitted to each of the **wheel housings**. The pressure of the oil forces the brake shoes or disks into contact with the wheels and slows them down.

The electrical system is a vital part of a modern car, and failures in any part of the system are among the most frequent causes of breakdowns. A battery provides power for starting, and for the lights when the car is parked. When the engine is running, it drives a dynamo or alternator which keeps the battery fully charged.

A network of electrical wiring, called a **harness**, runs throughout the car. This carries electricity to all the points where it is needed such as headlights, side lights and braking lights. It provides power for the windscreen wipers, and in some cars to open and close the windows or sun-roof. Electricity is also needed for the car radio or cassette player.

In some modern cars, electricity is needed to operate the microcomputers which tell the driver how much fuel is being used and how well the mechanical systems are functioning. This means that the silicon chip, one of our most recent inventions, has joined some of our oldest in making today's cars work well.

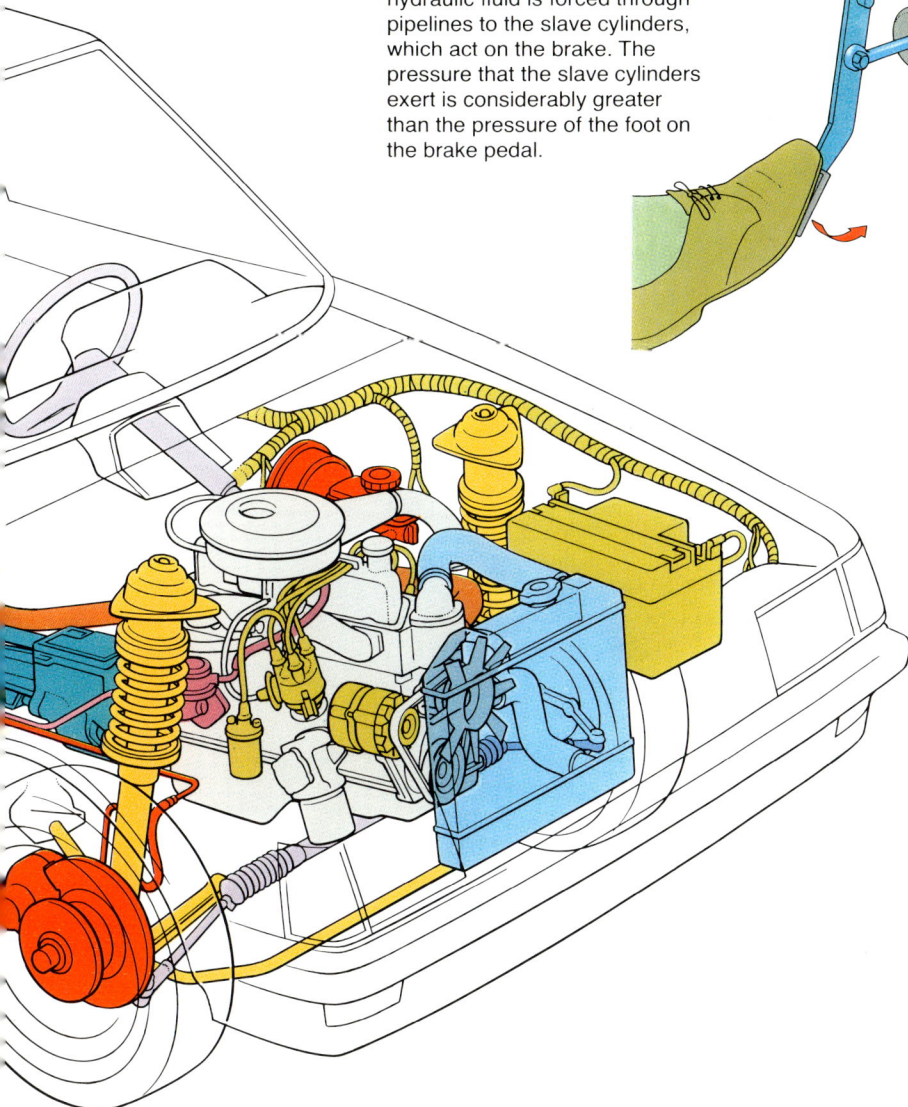

Wheels and tyres

The 'penny farthing' was an awkward machine to ride but was very popular in its day. It was designed in 1870 by James Stanley of Coventry, England. The rider sat high up, pedalling the large front wheel directly.

ANYONE WANTING to find out about wheels in the modern world could do no better than start with an ordinary bicycle. The **bicycle** has wheels of several different types and sizes. It also has gears, brakes and tyres like other forms of transport, though of a simpler kind. In many countries the bicycle is the most popular type of road vehicle. Perhaps the land is flat, the weather is generally fine, or the people are mostly not wealthy enough to afford motorized transport. A bicycle, in this case, is just what they need. It is cheap, needs no fuel and can be stored in a small space. It can also be ridden on roads with poor surfaces.

The earliest bicycles were nothing more than expensive toys for rich people. To use one of these early machines, sometimes called a 'dandy-horse' or 'hobby-horse', must have been uncomfortable. With no proper seat, and no pedals, the rider had to move along by pushing against the ground, first with one foot and then the other.

In 1839 a Scotsman named Macmillan invented a form of pedal-driven hobby-horse. The first, popular pedal-cycles, however, appeared in the 1860s. In Paris, Pierre and Ernest Michaux fitted pedals to the front wheel of a heavy machine they called a **velocipede**, (from the Latin 'swift-footed'). Some cyclists nicknamed it the 'boneshaker'. But one turn of the pedals meant only one turn of the wheels. To improve performance, some later bicycles were made with very large road wheels. The sensible answer was to use pedals on a toothed wheel (a **chain wheel**) connected by chain to a much smaller wheel with fewer teeth (a **sprocket**), fixed to the rear road wheel. This was first done about 1880. Shortly afterwards, bicycles began to look much as they do today, with two equal-sized wheels and a metal tubing frame.

All wheels are affected by **friction**. This is a force which tends to stop things moving. To help modern cycle wheels turn freely, their centres, or hubs, contain a number of hard,

Advanced design and technology have resulted in modern bicycles that are capable of withstanding very rough treatment. This in turn has led to the growth of a new sport, bicycle motocross, better known as BMX.

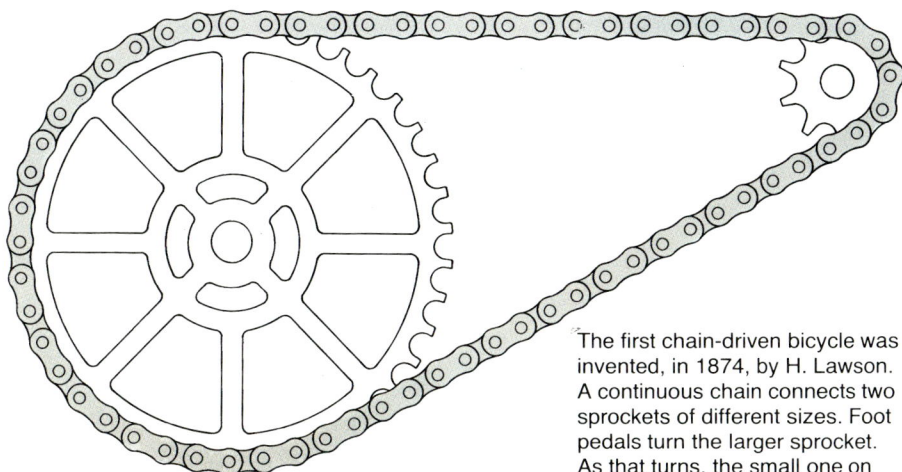

The first chain-driven bicycle was invented, in 1874, by H. Lawson. A continuous chain connects two sprockets of different sizes. Foot pedals turn the larger sprocket. As that turns, the small one on the rear wheel turns faster. The rear wheel then spins at the same rate as the small sprocket.

Cut away of a ballrace (right). Bearings are essential to the smooth performance of any wheel. They allow it to turn around its hub with the minimum of friction. The hard steel balls are lubricated with oil.

The wide tyres of Formula 1 racing cars have a very short life compared to those of standard motor cars. Their width and design offer good cornering power and grip, but a lot of rubber ends up on the track.

shiny steel balls. These ball bearings run in a tiny track called a **ball race**. In each bicycle wheel there are two races. You can easily make a simple model. Take two identical saucers, preferably unbreakable, and about fifteen marbles all of the same size. Put one saucer face downwards on a flat surface. Place the marbles on the bottom of the saucer, inside the little rim. Now put the second saucer carefully, right way up, on top of the marbles. If everything balances, a heavy book rested on the top saucer should revolve smoothly.

Even with ball bearings, a bicycle wheel will turn better if it has a lubricant. Friction literally means 'rubbing', and rubbing causes wear and heat. A lubricant is a substance which makes things more slippery, and able to slide against each other freely. Oil and grease are the most common. They are liquids, but graphite, found in pencil leads, is a solid often used as a lubricant.

Strangely enough, wheels cannot do without friction to work properly. How can this be? If it were not for friction, stopping a moving wheel would be impossible. With road vehicles, putting on the brake causes pads of hard-wearing material to rub against part of the wheel. This part, in most bicycles, is the outside edge of the wheel, just next to the tyre. In many motorcycles and cars it is a metal disk set around the centre of the wheel.

Until the 1870s, bicycle wheels were like those of most other forms of transport. They had wooden spokes, wooden rims and solid tyres.

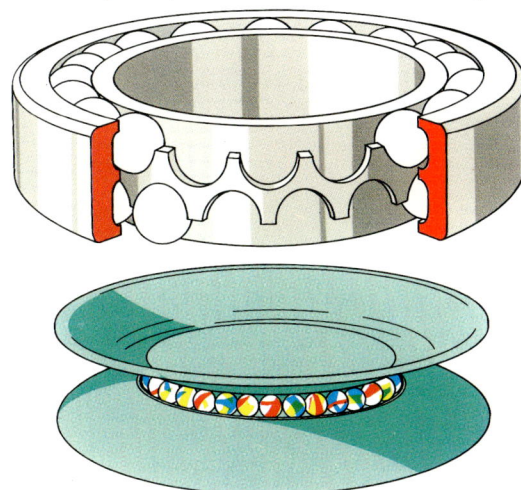

Two saucers separated by marbles will enable the top saucer to spin freely, whilst the lower one remains stationary.

Every bump in the uneven roads of those days was felt by the rider. The introduction of thin wire spokes helped to make riding a little more comfortable. These gave cycle wheels a slight springiness. But for proper protection against uneven road surfaces, cyclists had to wait for the appearance of **pneumatic** (air-filled) tyres. As far back as 1845, they had been tried out on the wheels of a horse-drawn carriage. John Boyd Dunlop, a Scotsman, re-invented tyres of this kind in 1888. His experiments showed that, given the same push, a wheel with an air-filled tyre would travel farther and quicker than one fitted with a solid tyre. Within a few years, all cycles were fitted with pneumatic tyres. Their use on cars, and especially trucks and buses, came much later.

With tyres, friction again has a part to play. The tread, or pattern of grooves, on a tyre helps a wheel to get a grip, even on wet or loose surfaces. A warm or slightly sticky tyre can do the same. This is why Grand Prix drivers have a 'warming-up' lap before a race starts.

35

Ships and the propeller

A STRANGE TUG-OF-WAR took place one day in 1845. It was a contest between two steamships staged by the British Navy. One was HMS *Rattler*, a ship designed by the famous engineer Brunel and fitted with a screw propeller. The other was a merchant ship, the *Alecto*, equipped with paddle-wheels, like most steamships of those times. Both ships were of about the same size, with engines of the same power. The tug-of-war was won by HMS *Rattler*. As a result, it is said, the use of screw propellers was adopted by the British Navy.

In fact the test was a little unfair. Under normal conditions, paddle-wheels worked as well as screw propellers, but they could be easily damaged by enemy gunfire or bad weather. Rough weather could also cause steering troubles. If a ship rolled, one of its paddle-wheels could come right out of the water. This would make the other wheel turn the ship round to one side.

In its earliest form, the screw propeller was shaped rather like the screws used to fasten pieces of wood together. This is not surprising,

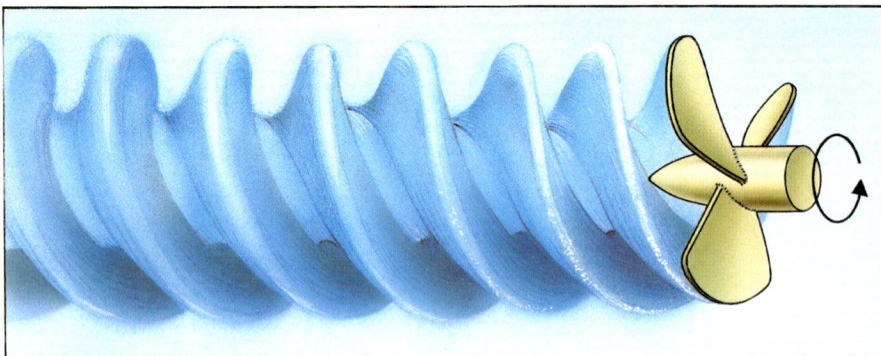

as when a propeller turns, it screws its way into the water and the thrust takes the whole ship forward with it. One of the first screw steamers, Francis Smith's *Archimedes*, built in 1838, had such a propeller, like a spiral with two complete turns. During the trial run half of the spiral was broken off by accident. To everyone's astonishment, this made the propeller work much better than before.

From then onward, ships' propellers were made in a shape similar to that which they have today – like the moving part of an electric fan. Brunel used a propeller of this shape on the first ocean going screw steamer *Great Britain*. Well

(top) The *Great Eastern* before its launch in 1857. In the foreground is the massive brake drum, used to slow the ship's movement during the launch. Launching involved a work force of over one thousand men.

The propeller (above) gives a ship movement by its screw-type action through water. The curved shape of the blades forces the water backwards, resulting in forward motion.

Compare the size of this four-bladed ship's propeller (right) with the step-ladder alongside.

over a century after being launched, this ship can still be seen in a dock in Bristol, England. Brunel's next iron ship, the gigantic *Great Eastern* built in 1857, was driven chiefly by paddle-wheels, but had a 9-m screw propeller too, with its own separate engine. For emergency use, and to save fuel, there were sails as well. The *Great Eastern* was 210 m long. No larger ship was built anywhere until 1899.

The *Shin Aitoku Maru* is the world's first sailing tanker. In addition to its energy-saving engine it has two sails which are operated by means of a microcomputer to achieve maximum power gain.

Sadly, the high cost of building and launching such a huge ship caused Brunel endless worry. His health broke down, and he died in 1859.

Modern ships' propellers have three or four blades. These are not flat, but twisted. The amount of twist is called the **pitch angle**. Some propellers are made of cast iron, but usually a material is used which resists rust, such as manganese bronze, or a special type of steel. A ship's propeller must be carefully designed, or bubbles of water vapour called cavities will form near the blades as they revolve. When these bubbles burst against the blades, they will gradually wear them away. The size and pitch angle of a propeller's blades depend on the power of the ship's engines and the speed at which they are run.

Nowadays many ships have large diesel engines. These are not usually connected directly to the propellers. They turn them by means of gear wheels, as ships' propellers revolve fairly slowly, at something between 80 and 120 times per minute. A less common arrangement is to use the diesel engines to produce electricity. This powers electric motors connected to the propellers.

Steam engines are also used in ocean-going ships. A few of them are still **reciprocating engines**, the kind in which pistons are moved to and fro by steam. Although old-fashioned, they are reliable and turn at a suitably slow speed for ships' propellers. Modern steamships use steam turbine engines. In these, jets of high-pressure steam push against small blades set round the edge of a large wheel, in much the same way as water turns the wheel in an old watermill. As with diesel engines, gear wheels connect the turbines to the propellers. Charles Parsons, one of the inventors of the steam turbine, demonstrated how well it worked in 1897 by interrupting a Naval Review held in honour of Queen Victoria. His boat, *Turbinia*, rushed between the lines of British warships at over 60 kph, too fast to be caught.

A modern ship normally has several engines. One or more of them may be shut down for repairs at sea, or if less power is needed. Most ships' engines run on oil. A search is now on for ways to save fuel. The USA and USSR have tried out nuclear-powered surface ships. Less expensive is the Japanese experiment of fitting a merchant ship with sails to assist the engines – hardly a new idea!

Ships are constructed in two main stages. First, the hull is built, section by section. Then it is launched and taken by tugs to the fitting-out basin for completion.

Balloons and airships

BALLOONS were the world's first successful flying machines. Joseph and Etienne Montgolfier were French brothers who ran a factory which made paper. In September 1783 a hot air balloon made by them was shown to a large crowd including the King and Queen of France. The balloon rose to a height of over 500 m. It carried three passengers – a sheep, a cockerel and a duck. After an eight-minute flight of some 4 km, the animals landed safely. Two months later another Montgolfier balloon, 23 m tall, carried the first human passengers into the air. This flight lasted twenty-five minutes. The two travellers kept the balloon flying by putting straw on to a fire in an iron basket hung in the opening at the bottom of it.

While the Montgolfiers used hot air to lift their balloons, another French team of inventors was experimenting with a newly discovered gas. This was hydrogen, which is lighter than normal air. In December 1783 these inventors, Jacques Charles and the Robert brothers, launched their own manned balloon. It was filled with hydrogen and made of rubber-coated silk. A great success, it travelled 50 km.

The French brothers, Joseph and Etienne Montgolfier, designed and built the first passenger-carrying hot air balloon. It made its maiden flight in September 1783 with three passengers aboard–a sheep, a cockerel and a duck. On 21st November in the same year, the Montgolfier brothers demonstrated the first manned flight. Two travellers took to the air from the Bois de Boulogne in Paris and made an aerial journey of 8km in twenty-five minutes. The following week, the first flight in a hydrogen-filled balloon was made. Since then, both gas and hot air balloons have been used for many sporting, military and scientific purposes.

Many early hot air balloons had been damaged by fire. Balloonists now began to choose the new gas, hydrogen, as it seemed safer and more efficient.

By 1800, balloon flights by male and female 'aeronauts' were a popular attraction. Planned air travel was still impossible, however. Round balloons can only go in the direction the wind blows. A French general named Meusnier realized as early as 1784 that to be **dirigible** (steerable), a balloon needs three things. It must have the shape of an egg or sausage, a propeller driven by an engine and some way of keeping its shape.

There are three types of dirigible balloon, or airship – as it is usually called. All three types have **fins** and **elevators** at the rear end to steer and control height. Non-rigid or pressure airships keep their shape chiefly because of the gas inside them. If this escapes, they sag or even collapse. Semi-rigid airships use a long, stiff framework, or keel, along the underside of the balloon to help maintain their shape. Rigid airships, as their name suggests, also have a framework, made of girders. These are attached to circular frames, sometimes known as rings. In a rigid airship, the gas is in about fifteen separate balloons contained inside the framework.

The world's first airship, flown by Henri Giffard in 1852, was non-rigid. Almost all the airships flying today are non-rigids. In the two World Wars, the Allies used them to protect ships against submarine attack. Now non-rigid airships carry TV cameras to record news or

Having devised a method of air travel, the next step for the early flyers was to make an aircraft that was dirigible (steerable). The world's first airship was flown in 1852 by its inventor, Henri Giffard. Although today we seldom see airships, they have many advantages over other aircraft. They are clean, quiet and can hover. The Skyship (above) can carry up to twelve passengers and two flight crew in the payload compartment. This is known as the gondola (below). and is suspended from the hull.

sporting events, or advertisements for products such as tyres. People sometimes call these airships 'blimps'. Why is this? One story tells that, in the first World War, a British naval officer once flicked his finger against the gas-bag of a non-rigid airship. It gave out a noise which sounded rather like 'blimp'.

Semi-rigid airships were chiefly made in Italy and France. The best known semi-rigid types were 'Norge' and 'Italia' used by the Italian Umberto Nobile in the 1920s to explore the Arctic. Germany became famous for its rigid airships, which were invented by a German, Count Zeppelin. These were enormous. Over 200 m long, they were the biggest flying machines the world has ever seen. For several years the only aircraft able to carry passengers regularly across the Atlantic were Zeppelin airships.

Not many airships can be seen today. They turned out to be less successful than planes. They were very large and flew very slowly, so they were affected by bad weather. The hydrogen used in most of them was inflammable and caused accidents. Despite their size they carried few passengers.

Even so, some people believe that airships have a future. They fly fairly quietly and do not use much fuel or pollute the air. Airships can hover like helicopters and stay up for many hours. **Helium** gas, which is not dangerous like hydrogen, is now more widely available to fill them. Plans have been drawn up to build giant cargo-carriers, bigger even than Zeppelins. But will airships ever be cheap enough to run at a profit? That is a question that only the future can answer.

Early gliders and aircraft

THE TWO WRIGHT BROTHERS, Wilbur and Orville, are given the honour of being the first men to fly successfully in a powered aeroplane. As bicycle makers, they were skilled in the use of tools. Even so, it is remarkable that they were able to design and build both the aeroplane and its engine. Success did not come to them without much hard work and many disappointments. Their successful powered flight in 1903 followed three years of flying full-size gliders. The most important lesson they learned was that an aeroplane had to be fully under the control of its pilot. The aeroplane had to be able to bank, climb and dive like a bird.

In 1905, the two Wright brothers flew their *Flyer III*. This was the world's first practical aeroplane, since it could be banked, turned, circled and flown in figures of eight. Also, on two occasions, flights lasted for over half an hour.

But where in history did all this begin? We must ignore the tower jumpers and the 'flappers'. Most of these unfortunate people leapt to their death with tiny wings strapped to their arms, and not one of them really flew. Leonardo da Vinci sketched designs for a flapping wing machine in the sixteenth century. In fact, human beings do not have enough muscle to make such a device work.

It was Sir George Cayley (1773–1857) who

The American brothers, Wilbur and Orville Wright, spent three years experimenting with gliders, learning wing control and lateral balancing. They eventually made the first successful powered flight, in December 1903, at Kitty Hawk, North Carolina. Wilbur is the pilot of the glider *(right)* on a flight in 1901.

Sir George Cayley was the first scientist to work on the basic principles of mechanical flight. In 1809, he published a paper called *On Aerial Navigation*. In this paper, he laid the foundations from which aviation developed. He was the first person to understand how birds fly, and he designed a number of flying machines.

invented the modern type of aeroplane, that is, an aeroplane with fixed wings, a tail and movable control surfaces. Sir George was a wealthy Englishman who lived in Yorkshire, England. In 1810 he had published his study of **aerodynamics**, the science of movement in air. In 1849 he built a full-size triplane glider, with three sets of wings. This was launched from a hillside, with a ten-year-old boy on board. The glider floated off the ground for a few metres.

The first, proper, manned glider flight was made in 1853, when Sir George's coachman was launched from a hillside. Although the controls were locked, the glider flew across a small valley. At the end of the flight, the coachman shouted back across the valley, 'Please, Sir George, I wish to give notice. I was hired to drive, not to fly.'

Henson and Stringfellow deserve a mention. Although they never built a full-size machine they received much publicity. Pictures of their designs appeared in many books and magazines. Henson had grand ideas for a steam-driven airline to fly to India. Pictures show its imagined arrival in Egypt with the pyramids in sight. Stringfellow built a large steam-driven model monoplane in 1848, which almost flew.

Around 1857, a Frenchman, Captain J. M. Le Bris, built a large glider shaped like an albatross. According to accounts, it was launched from a farm cart driven downhill. It crashed and the brave captain broke a leg.

A Russian, steam-driven monoplane was

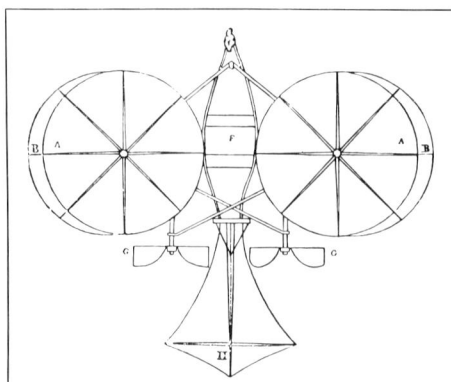

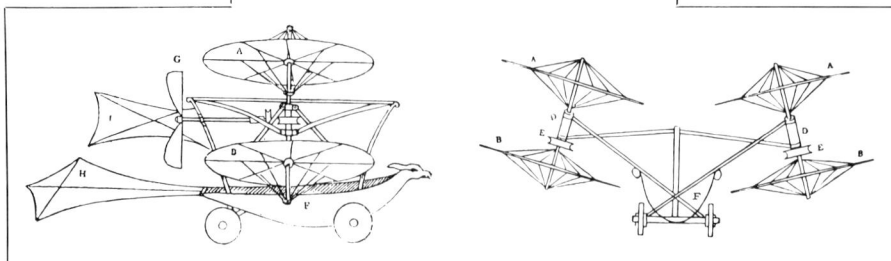

Sir George Cayley *(above)* is considered to be the true inventor of the aeroplane.

One of Cayley's great admirers was the English engineer William Samuel Henson (1812-88). Henson had grand ideas of designing steam-driven airliners that would fly to India. None of his designs ever flew, but the picture *(above)* shows the imagined arrival of one of these airliners in Egypt.

Despite the efforts of the other aviators the first controlled and piloted glider was built by the German engineer, Otto Lilienthal. He made many flights between 1891 and 1896, but finally crashed and was killed.

built in 1884. Designed by A. F. Mozhaiski, it was powered by an English engine. Launched from a specially built 'ski-jump' ramp, this, too, made only a short hop.

The first machine to leave the ground under its own power was the *Ede*. Built by Clement Ader, a Frenchman, this machine only made a short, powered hop.

Perhaps believing that bigger must be better, an Englishman, Sir Hiram Maxim, built an enormous steam-powered biplane in 1894, at a substantial cost. Testing took place at Baldwyn's Park in Kent, England. It was another failure.

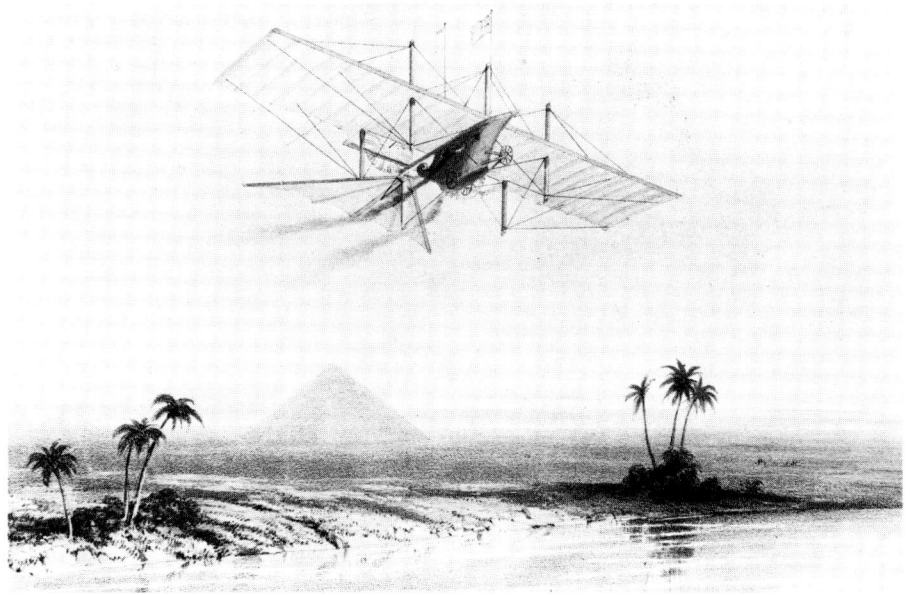

All machines of this type were handicapped by the weight of steam engine and boiler. Also, little thought had been given to control of the machines in the air.

Real progress was now taking place with gliders. A German, Otto Lilienthal (1848–96), built the first hang-glider. He believed in carrying out his experiments in the air, and even had an artificial hill built near Berlin. This meant he could launch himself into the wind in any direction. He made hundreds of flights in monoplane and biplane gliders. Sadly, he was killed in 1896, when his monoplane glider met a strong gust of wind and **stalled**. It side-slipped and crashed to the ground.

Lilienthal's achievements did much to encourage others. Captain F. Ferber in France, Octave Chanute in the United States and Percy Pilcher in England all built gliders. In the year that Lilienthal met his death, Percy Pilcher flew his glider called the *Hawk*. This very advanced glider had a wheeled undercarriage and was launched by a towline. He was working on a petrol engine to power an aeroplane of his design when he, too, was killed in 1899.

Octave Chanute was also successful in designing gliders. He made seven hundred safe flights, some of up to 100 m. In 1900 the Wright brothers made contact with Chanute. Although now aged 68, he gave them great encouragement with their experiments. The Wright gliders differed from the Lilienthal gliders. The pilot lay on the lower wing and moved control surfaces to manoeuvre the craft. This method led to success, and with the addition of the petrol engine driving two propellers, here was the world's first practical aeroplane.

How aeroplanes fly

A CAR, as it travels, is supported by the road beneath its wheels. A ship steaming across the ocean is supported by the water around its hull. But can thin air really support a Boeing 747 Jumbo jet in flight? It certainly does, and very successfully. The wings of the Boeing 747 and the airflow around them support all 360 tonnes of its mass.

Strange as it may seem, both the Boeing 747 and a micro-light aeroplane have the same kind of forces acting on them. There are always four forces which have to be in balance for any aeroplane to fly straight and level. Think of them as two pairs of forces, **lift** and weight and **thrust** and **drag**. Lift has to overcome the weight of the aeroplane. Thrust has to overcome the drag.

The four forces that act on an aircraft in flight. Drag is caused by air resistance, thrust by the propeller (or jet engine), weight by gravity, and lift by the airflow over the wings.

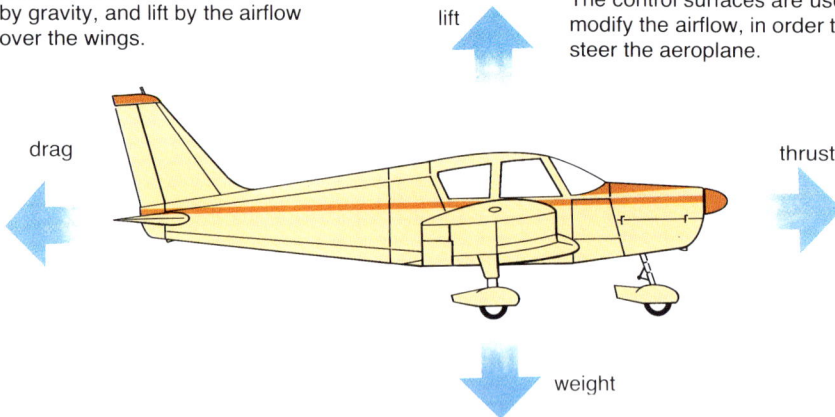

The aerofoil section *(top)* of a wing generates lift as it moves through the air.

The control surfaces are used to modify the airflow, in order to steer the aeroplane.

Lift is an upwards force and supports the aeroplane in flight. It is produced by the airflow over the wings. Each wing of an aeroplane has a special shape which is called an **aerofoil**. An aerofoil has a top and bottom surface each with a different curve, or **camber**. There is usually more camber on the top surface. A curved surface can give much more lift than a flat one.

In normal flight the airflow over the wings is smooth *(left)*. Below a certain speed *(right)* the airflow becomes turbulent resulting in a loss of lift. The aircraft will then stall and drop suddenly.

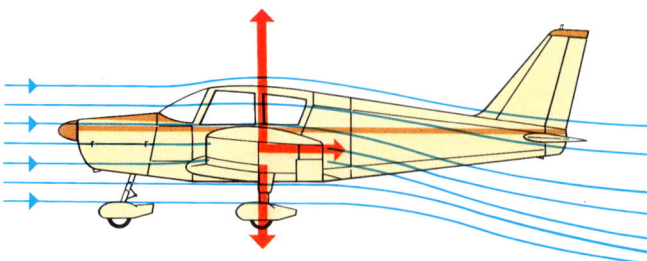

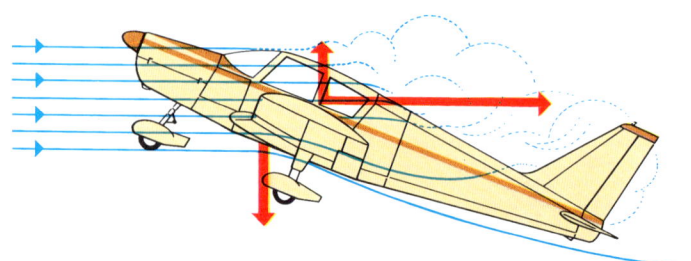

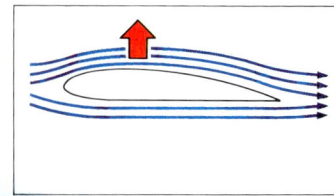

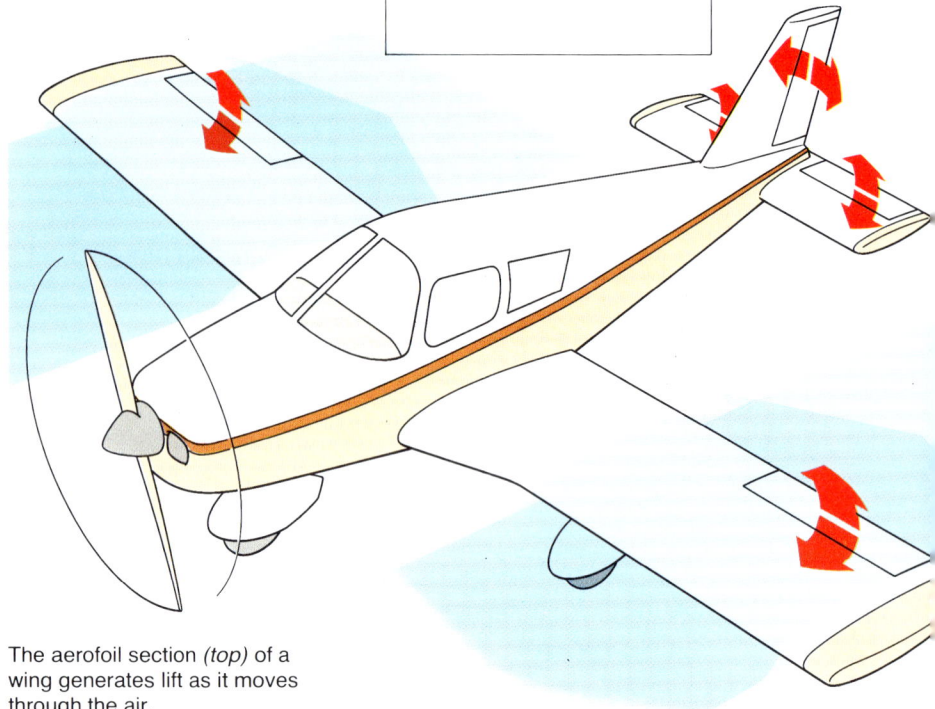

Wings are inclined upwards at a slight angle and are built on to the **fuselage**, or body, of the aeroplane. This means the front, or leading, edge is slightly higher than the trailing edge. As the aerofoil moves through the air the airflow divides to pass over and under it. The air striking the underside of the aerofoil produces an upward force, but only one-third of a wing's lift is produced this way. Most of the lift comes from the airflow over the top of the wing. The curved top surface is longer than the underside. The airflow over the top, therefore, has to travel further. Because of this, it speeds up and the pressure becomes less. This lowering of pressure gives two-thirds of all the lift. It is called the **Bernouilli effect**, named after the Swiss scientist Daniel Bernouilli.

Anything moving through the air experiences drag, the slowing-down effect that air has on anything moving. This is why you do not go on and on increasing speed when you freewheel your bicycle downhill. The Boeing 747 has four powerful gas-turbine jet engines to overcome drag. But, even so, there is a maximum speed of 969 kph. Some aeroplanes, including micro-lights, use propellers to give thrust.

An aeroplane has to be able to **manoeuvre**. This means it has to be able to change height and direction at the command of the pilot. The control system used by most aeroplanes depends on hinged control surfaces on the trailing edges of the wings, tailplane and fin.

The **ailerons** are the hinged surfaces on the trailing edge of each wing and they control rolling to left or right. The pilot operates them by moving his control column to left or right. They are also used, together with the **rudder**, to make a banked turn. Like a bicycle, an aircraft turns by **banking**. Ailerons are always arranged so that as one aileron goes up, the other goes down.

The rudder is hinged to the trailing edge of the fin. It is normally used together with the ailerons to make a banked turn. The pilot moves the rudder with foot controls.

The **elevators** are hinged surfaces on the trailing edge of the tailplane. They are used to make the aeroplane climb or dive. The control column also works the elevators. The pilot pushes the control column forward to dive, and pulls it towards him to climb.

In order to land safely, an aeroplane has to fly as slowly as possible without stalling. An aeroplane stalls when it slows down to a speed where the airflow no longer flows smoothly over the wings. When this happens the wings no longer produce enough lift. The aeroplane then begins to fall out of the sky. A pilot is trained to recover his aeroplane from a stall if he

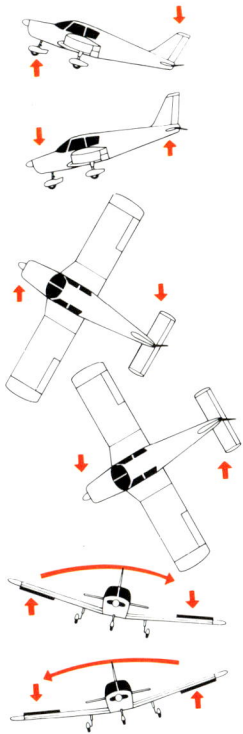

The control surfaces include ailerons on the wings, and elevators and rudders at the tail. Pitch (top) is controlled by the elevators, yaw (centre) by the rudder, and roll (lower) by the ailerons.

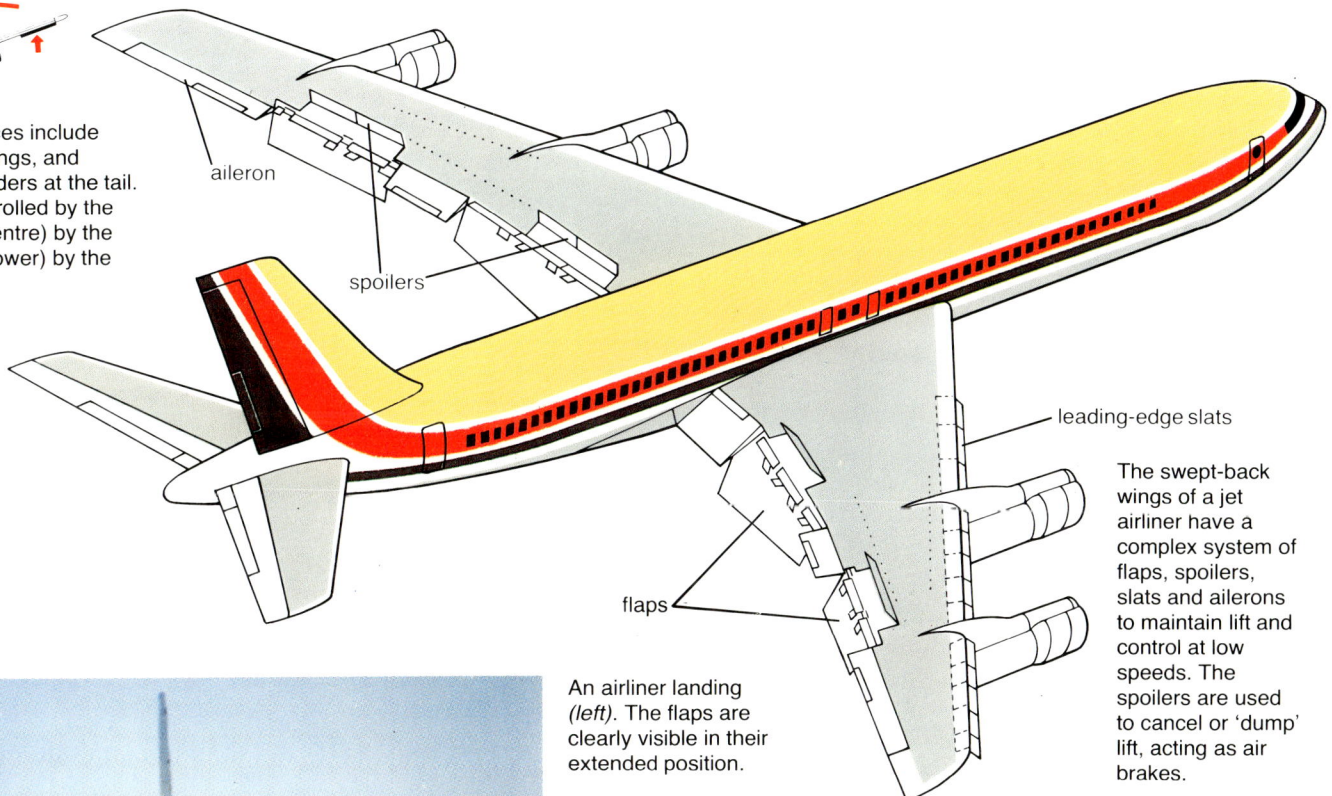

aileron

spoilers

leading-edge slats

The swept-back wings of a jet airliner have a complex system of flaps, spoilers, slats and ailerons to maintain lift and control at low speeds. The spoilers are used to cancel or 'dump' lift, acting as air brakes.

flaps

An airliner landing (left). The flaps are clearly visible in their extended position.

is at a safe height, but stalling near the ground results in a crash. To be able to fly slowly and safely, modern aircraft have **flaps** and leading-edge slots. Flaps are hinged surfaces on each wing, between the aileron and the fuselage. Flaps are always lowered together to increase the lift. They are used for take-off and landing. Leading-edge slots can be opened to smooth out the airflow over the wings at slow speed.

The next time you see an aeroplane close up, see if you can spot the control surfaces, the flaps and the slots.

The jet engine

NOWADAYS modern jet aircraft are a familiar sight in the sky and we take them for granted. Some people tend to think of jet propulsion as a new invention. It was, however, already an old idea when the German Heinkel HE 178 became the first aeroplane in the world to fly, powered by a jet engine. The date was 24th August 1939.

If we ask who invented the jet engine, the truthful answer is that we do not know. Sir Isaac Newton deserves some of the credit because his Third Law of Motion states, 'To every action, there is an equal and opposite **reaction**'. What does that mean? Imagine yourself standing on roller skates, and using all your force to throw a large stone forward. At that moment you, on your skates, feel an equal force pushing you in the opposite direction, that is to say backwards.

An aeroplane is propelled forward by just the same kind of reaction-force, whether it is powered by a propeller or by a jet engine. The propeller throws back a broad column of air fairly slowly, and the jet engine throws back a thin column of hot gas at high speed. In either case the reaction forces the aeroplane in the opposite direction.

It is believed that Isaac Newton thought of propelling a carriage by a jet of steam in 1687. In 1867 two Englishmen, Butler and Edwards

A simple way of showing the theory of jet propulsion *(right)*, provided the skater can keep his balance.

Sir Frank Whittle.

The Gloster E 28/29 *(below)* in which Whittle's turbo-jet engine flew in 1941.

patented a delta-wing aeroplane driven by steam jets. This aeroplane looked very much like a paper dart. If only they could have seen the Concorde!

Charles Parsons built the first successful steam-turbine engine for use in ships in 1896. He was also very interested in gas-turbines, but progress was delayed by the lack of suitable metals. Inside a gas-turbine engine there are very high temperatures which can melt normal steel.

Then in 1937, in an old factory at Rugby, England, a Royal Air Force officer named Frank Whittle ran his new turbo-jet aero engine. It leaked fuel which frequently caught fire. On one occasion it ran at too high a speed and blew up. Neither gas-turbines nor jet propulsion were invented by Frank Whittle but he must receive credit for making the world's first successful turbo-jet.

Meanwhile, totally unknown to Whittle, a certain Pabst von Ohain was also working on a turbo-jet. Although Frank Whittle's was the first to run, Von Ohain's engine was the first into the air, in the Heinkel 178. It was not until 15th May 1941 that the Whittle engine first flew. It was mounted in the tiny aeroplane, the E28/39, built by the Gloster Aircraft Company. It flew hundreds of times over the next five years, but the Heinkel 178 never flew again after 1939.

The type of engine which now powers all civil and most military jet aircraft is the gas-turbine. This is an air-breathing engine (not a rocket) which burns **kerosine**.

With the engine running, air is drawn into the **compressor**. The compressor, driven by the turbine and turning at high speed, has a series of many moving and fixed blades. The blades are shaped like small wings to sweep the air rearwards. By the time the air reaches the combustion chamber it is travelling at just below the speed of sound. The air is also at high pressure and very hot.

The kerosine fuel is sprayed into the combustion chamber and burns as a continuous fierce flame. The very hot gases produced are then expanded as they pass through the turbine. Once past the turbine, the hot gases rush out of the exhaust nozzle. The reaction to this stream or jet of hot gases provides the thrust to drive the aeroplane forward.

The turbine is necessary to drive the com-

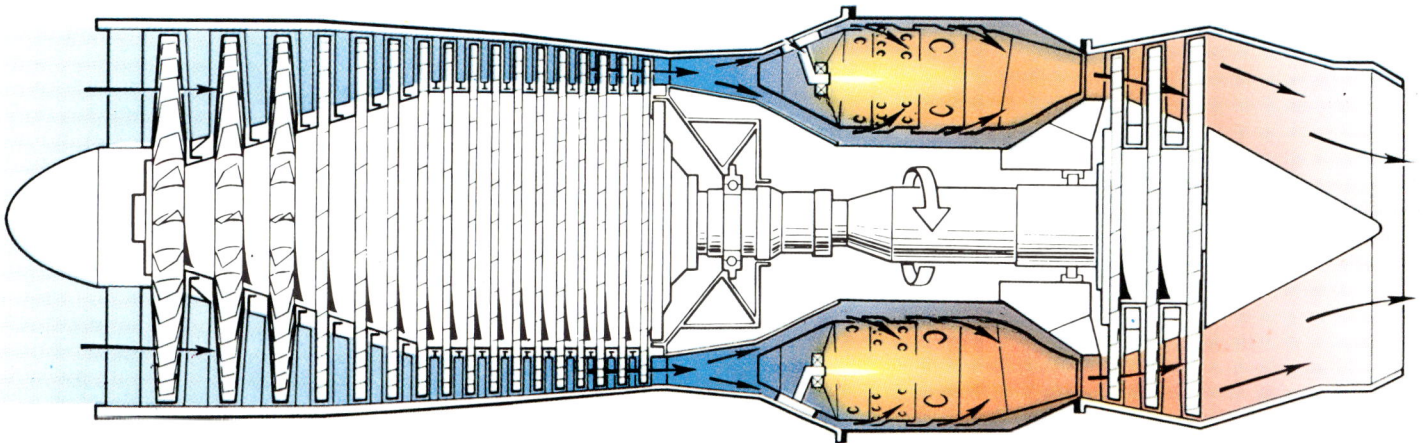

A gas turbine engine *(above)* sucks in air and uses it to provide thrust. As the air passes through the engine it is accelerated and heated, eventually being forced out as a powerful jet.

(top) The wide-bodied McDonnell Douglas DC-10 airliner has three engines. The centre engine is positioned right through the base of the tail, and changing it involves dismantling the rear of the aircraft. This picture *(left)* of engineers standing inside the cowling of a dismantled DC-10 engine gives a good indication of its size.

pressor. It consists of one or more disks with numerous wing-like blades fixed to their edges. Note that a turbo-prop engine has an extra turbine to drive the propeller.

The gas-turbine has grown enormously in power output since Frank Whittle's first experiments. The engine which powered the little Gloster E28/39 had a thrust of just 390 kg. This compares with the 17 260 kg of thrust produced by each one of the Concorde's four engines.

Helicopters

A HELICOPTER is an aeroplane, but it is an aeroplane with a difference. It can hover, or hang, in the air, and it is able to do this because its wings are not fixed, but rotate. This means that they go around and around, driven by an engine. Because the wings of the helicopter are long, thin and rotate, they are known as **rotor-blades**.

Rotor-blades, like the wings of birds and the fixed wings of aeroplanes, have an aerofoil shape. When moving air meets the aerofoil, it divides, some flowing over the blade and some underneath. The air that flows over the top has further to go because the surface is curved. It therefore travels faster and this lowers the air pressure. The air flowing underneath moves more slowly, so the air pressure is higher. Since there is greater pressure below the aerofoil than above, the rotor-blade is forced upwards. We call this lift.

It is lift which enables birds, fixed-wing aeroplanes and helicopters to remain in the air. Birds and fixed-wing aeroplanes have to rush through the air for their wings to give lift. The

When a stream of air passes over an aerofoil, the air flowing over the upper surface travels faster than the air underneath. This makes the air pressure underneath higher than that above, which creates lift.

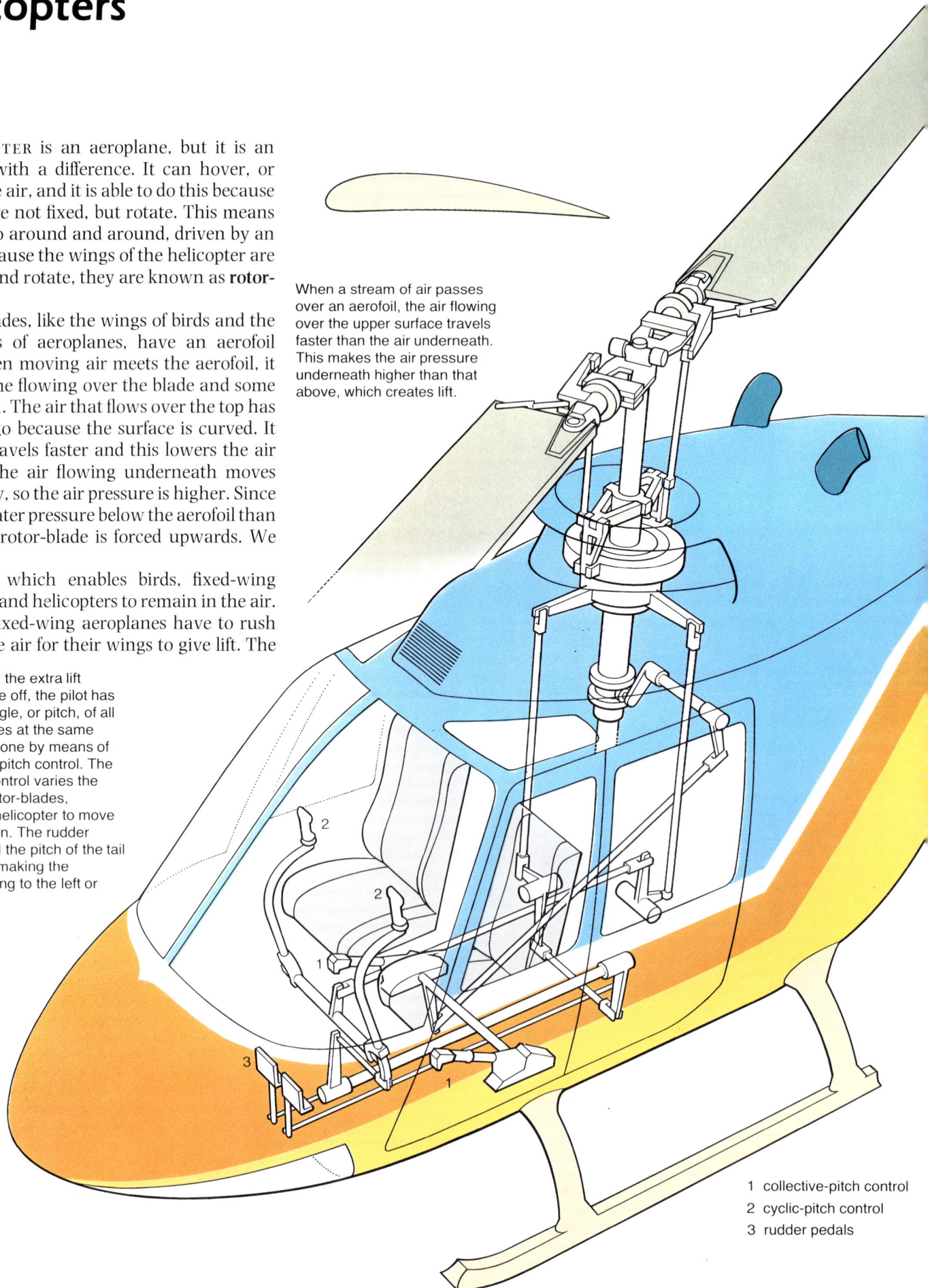

In order to get the extra lift needed to take off, the pilot has to alter the angle, or pitch, of all the rotor-blades at the same time. This is done by means of the collective-pitch control. The cyclic-pitch control varies the pitch of the rotor-blades, enabling the helicopter to move in any direction. The rudder pedals control the pitch of the tail rotor-blades, making the helicopter swing to the left or right.

1 collective-pitch control
2 cyclic-pitch control
3 rudder pedals

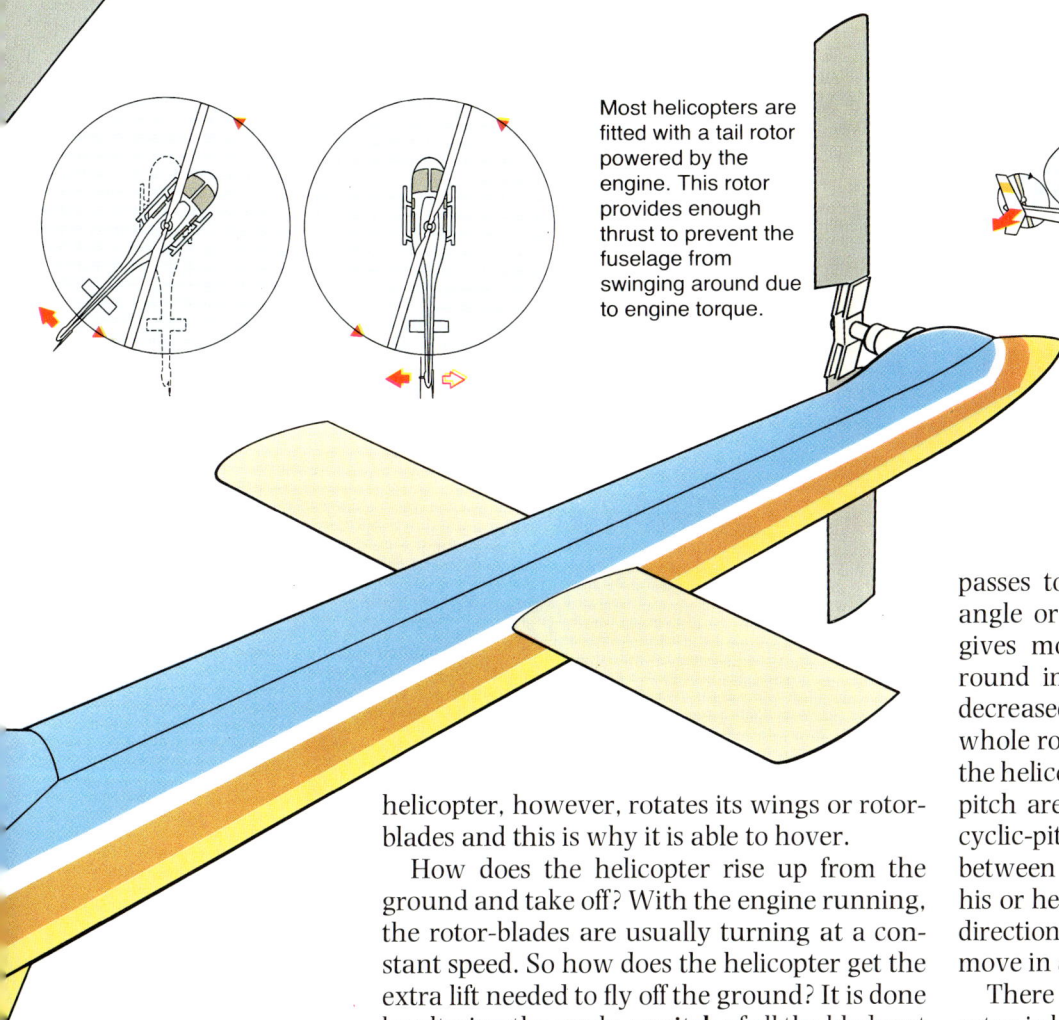

Most helicopters are fitted with a tail rotor powered by the engine. This rotor provides enough thrust to prevent the fuselage from swinging around due to engine torque.

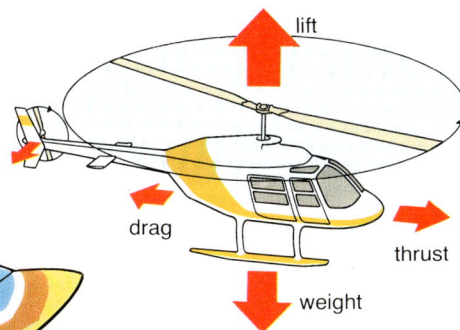

The four forces that act on a helicopter in flight are weight, lift, drag and thrust. The directions in which they act can be calculated and the helicopter is designed to take advantage of each of them.

(A) On take-off, the lift is greater than the weight and the helicopter climbs vertically; (B) lift equals weight, causing the helicopter to hover; (C) to move into forward flight the cyclic-pitch control is moved forwards and the lift increased to maintain level flight; (D) pulling the cyclic-pitch control back makes the helicopter move backwards; (E) on descent lift is less than weight.

helicopter, however, rotates its wings or rotor-blades and this is why it is able to hover.

How does the helicopter rise up from the ground and take off? With the engine running, the rotor-blades are usually turning at a constant speed. So how does the helicopter get the extra lift needed to fly off the ground? It is done by altering the angle, or **pitch** of all the blades at the same time. The pilot controls this using the collective pitch control. This is a lever held in the pilot's left hand. When the collective pitch lever is raised the lift of the rotor-blades increases. The helicopter now climbs. When the lever is lowered the lift decreases and the helicopter descends.

Helicopters can also travel forwards, sideways or even backwards. Fixed-wing aeroplanes have propellers or jets to give the **thrust** which pushes them through the air. The helicopter, like birds, has to use rotor-blades as wings to provide lift and to give forward movement. In a helicopter this is done by tilting the blades to give thrust. This could be done by tilting the whole rotor head. In fact it has been found much simpler to hinge each rotor-blade so that it can flap up or down.

To obtain forward flight extra lift is gained from each rotor-blade in turn. As each blade

passes towards the tail of the helicopter the angle or pitch of the blade is increased. This gives more lift. As each blade then sweeps round in front of the helicopter the pitch is decreased. Because the blades are hinged, the whole rotor is tilted forward. The result is that the helicopter moves forward. These changes of pitch are known as **cyclic-pitch** changes. The cyclic-pitch control is also a lever, sticking up between the pilot's knees. The pilot holds it in his or her right hand, and by moving it in any direction the pilot can make the helicopter move in any direction.

There is one further problem. When a main rotor is being rotated under power, a reaction tends to rotate the helicopter in the opposite direction. We call this reaction **engine torque**. To overcome this reaction most helicopters have a small tail rotor powered by the engine. This gives enough thrust to stop the fuselage from swinging round.

Suppose the pilot needs to alter the direction of flight? Both hands are already occupied with controls. The pilot's feet are free and these rest on a pair of pedals which control the pitch of the tail rotor-blades. By pushing on the left or right pedal the thrust of the tail rotor is altered, and this makes the helicopter swing to the left or right.

The pilot therefore has full control over the helicopter which can be made to move in any direction required and can also hover. Modern helicopters are easier to fly than some of the earlier types, but even so it takes great skill to fly these amazing machines.

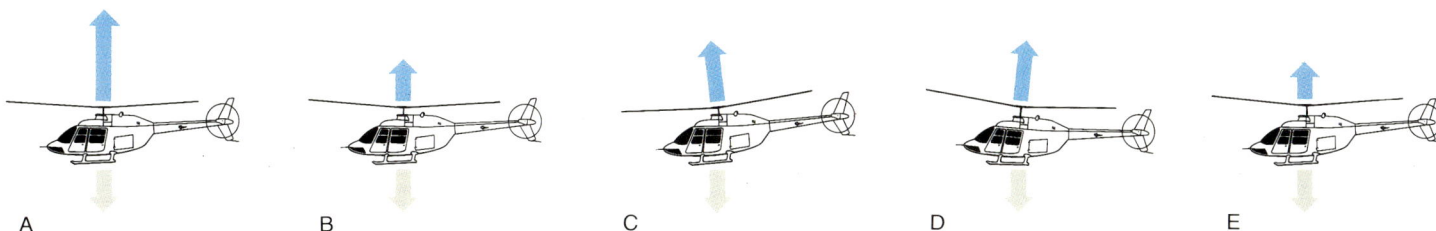

A   B   C   D   E

The birdmen

Soon after the first aircraft had flown successfully, people began to wonder how airmen could escape during a flight if anything went wrong. In 1783 a Frenchman, Sebastian Lenormand, had demonstrated the use of a parachute as a way of escaping from a tall, burning building. After this, a number of men had made parachute descents from balloons. These had been 'stunts', some of which proved unsuccessful. No one had thought that the parachute might have a serious use.

The early parachutes were really large umbrellas. Although modern parachutes are more complicated, they work on the same principle. When the parachutist pulls a cord, a large area of material unfolds in the air and takes the shape of an umbrella. This **canopy**, as it is known, attached to a harness worn by the parachutist, traps air and so resists the force of **gravity**. The first successful parachute descent from an aircraft was made in 1912, and, after this, parachutes became part of the flying gear of all air crew. However, training is needed to use a parachute. Therefore, once aircraft began to carry passengers, parachutes were supplied only to military fliers. Some modern military aircraft are fitted with **ejector seats**. If a pilot decides to abandon an aircraft, he presses a button and is thrown upwards, still in his seat, clear of the plane. The parachute then opens and lets him down to earth slowly and safely.

A square-rig parachute is easily steered and can move at a forward speed of about 40 kph. The extra control enables a jumper to land on a target the size of a basketball from a height of 3000 m.

Some people go parachuting as a sport, or to raise money for charity. Sky-diving, or 'free fall' parachuting, is often done by teams of people who let themselves fall as much as a kilometre or more before opening their parachutes. They often make patterns while they perform a kind of dance in space.

Gliding is another airborne sport. Gliders are aircraft without engines. They are made of wood, fabric or fibreglass, and are extremely light. They have narrow **fuselages** and large wing areas to increase their lift.

Although the Wright brothers are best known as the inventors of the first successful powered aircraft, they were also pioneers of gliding. Four years before their famous powered flight they had made their first trip in a glider. For many years they were the world record-holders for the longest glider flight, which lasted over two hours. If conditions are right, modern gliders can travel for several hundred kilometres.

Gliders cannot take off without help. Sometimes they are towed into the air by powered aircraft and then released. Alternatively, they can be launched by a cable-operated **winch**. Once launched, gliders rely on lift to keep them aloft on short flights. Pilots try to find **thermals**. These are rising currents of warm air. Once the

The sport of gliding is popular world-wide. The current long-distance record was set in April 1972 by Hans Werner Grosse of West Germany, who flew 1460.8 km from Lubeck to Biarritz.

To stay up in the air for a long period, a glider needs to make use of rising air currents, or thermals. A glider pilot has to know how thermals behave and where to look for them. Rising air also rotates, so a skilled pilot will turn the glider with the rising air, in order to gain maximum height.

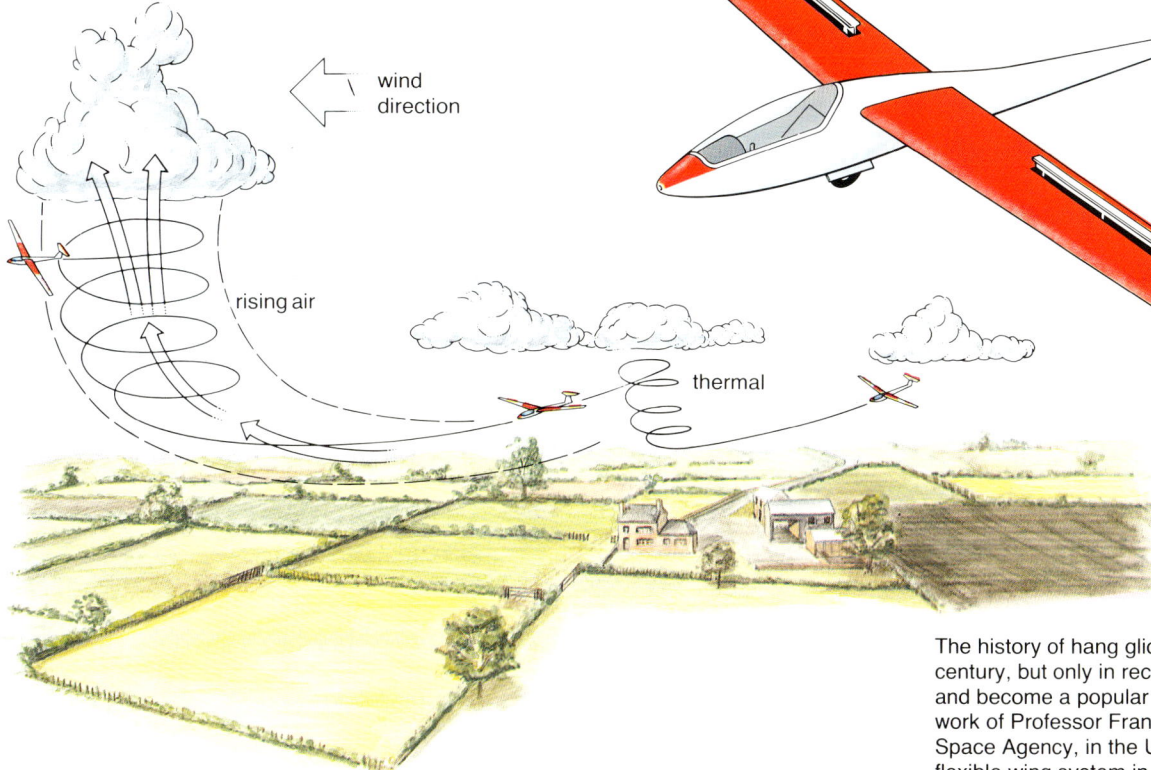

wind direction

rising air

thermal

The history of hang gliding dates from the nineteenth century, but only in recent years has it really developed and become a popular sport. This is largely due to the work of Professor Francis Rogallo of the National Space Agency, in the United States, who invented a flexible wing system in the 1950s.

glider finds a thermal, it is able to climb, and so make a longer flight. The glider climbs to the top of the thermal in a spiral and then glides slowly down in search of another. A glider has three main instruments, an altimeter, which indicates height, a **variometer**, which shows how fast the glider is gaining or losing height, and an airspeed indicator. The controls are similar to those of a light powered aircraft. There is a joystick to control climbing and diving, and pedals to operate the rudder.

Even lighter than the glider is the **hang-glider**, sometimes called the 'delta kite'. This is really no more than a large kite below which the pilot hangs. Hang-gliders are launched from hilltops or cliffs and rely on the upward currents of air to carry them along. Ordinary hang-gliders cannot stay airborne for very long, but some are now fitted with small motors and can make journeys of more than 100 km.

Will we ever be able to fly by using only our own power? Now that man-made materials, such as fibreglass, make it possible to build very light aircraft, we might, one day, be able to go for a flight using pedal-power. Several people have built aircraft with propellers turned by pedals, but the amount of effort needed is too exhausting to keep up for long.

Hydrofoils and hovercraft

IT IS MUCH EASIER to travel through air than through water. At the seaside, walking along the beach is normally faster than wading along knee-deep in the sea. If a boat has an engine, a great deal of its power is used in pushing the hull, or body of the boat, through the water. A boat whose hull is out of the water can travel more quickly. Hydrofoil boats and hovercraft are two answers to this problem of 'water resistance'.

As a hydrofoil boat gathers speed, it rises out of the water. Only its hydrofoils and its propeller remain below the surface. Hydrofoils are shaped like aircraft wings. The top surface is curved, while the bottom surface is flat. Water passes more quickly over the curved top than beneath the bottom. This reduces the water pressure on the top of the hydrofoils compared to the pressure from underneath. They rise, and take the boat with them. A similar thing happens with air and an aircraft wing.

As a hydrofoil increases speed, only its propeller and foils remain in the water. The foils are shaped like aircraft wings, so they produce lift. Friction is reduced enabling high speeds to be reached.

V-shaped foils (above) pierce the surface of the water and help to steady the craft. They are the most common form for passenger hydrofoils. Submerged foils (right) are more suited to rough sea conditions because their angle is adjustable. They are controlled by an autopilot.

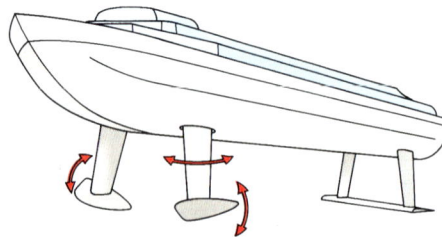

There are two main types of hydrofoil. 'V-foils' stick out of the water on both sides of the boat as it moves along at speed. The other kind of hydrofoil stays hidden under water. With this type, the angle of the foil can be changed while the boat is going, to suit different water conditions. A boat with underwater foils looks as if it is travelling on a set of legs.

Hydrofoils are not a new idea. In 1919 Alexander Graham Bell, more famous for in-

venting the telephone, tried out a hydrofoil boat on Lake Bras d'Or in Canada. Driven by two aircraft engines, it reached well over 100 kph. Present-day hydrofoil boats are used as ferries on lakes and rivers, or on short sea crossings. Both Norway and the USSR have built hydrofoil ferries, each of which can carry more than one hundred passengers.

Boats with hydrofoils do not make large waves behind them as they go along, because their hulls are out of the water. This means they cause less harm to river banks and other small boats they pass. But there are problems. A hydrofoil can be damaged by hitting a floating object and at a certain speed, around 90 kph, hydrofoils can break up. Hydrofoil boats work best in smooth water, and there seems to be a limit to the size one can make them. At present, few ocean-going hydrofoil ships have been built.

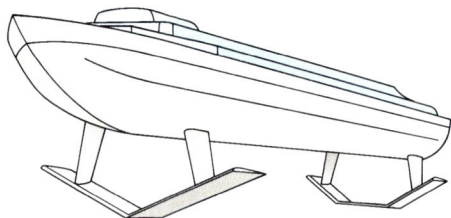

Unlike a hydrofoil, a hovercraft can travel over water or land. It is supported by a cushion of air which is contained by a tough, flexible skirt.

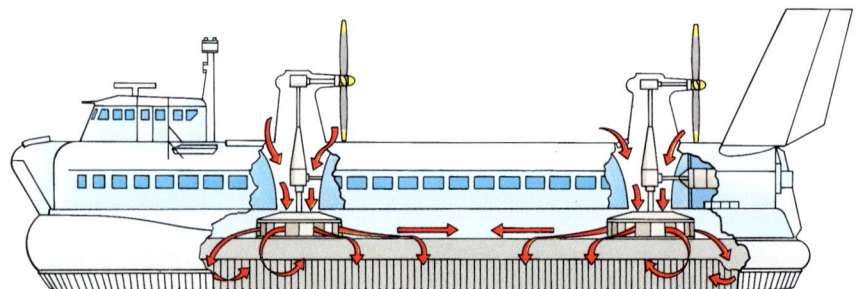

Place a sheet of paper on a smooth table-top. Blow under one edge of the paper, and it will float away over the table on a cushion of air. In a similar way, a hovercraft skims over water or land.

A hovercraft is sometimes known as an **air-cushion vehicle** (ACV). When it hovers just above the surface, it is supported by a cushion of air. As the air escapes from around the bottom of the hovercraft, it is replaced by powerful fans. To prevent too much air leaking out, a 'skirt' of material, which may be either stiff or flexible, is usually fitted round the base of the craft. In 1955 Sir Christopher Cockerell, a British engineer, thought up the idea of having powerful, downward air jets as a kind of skirt to keep the air-cushion in. He used simple things such as tin cans and a hair-drier in his experiments.

Thanks to Cockerell's 'air-curtain' idea, the construction of passenger-carrying hovercraft started. The first of these, the SRN-1, flew in 1959. Some ten years later, giant SRN-4s, many times bigger, began to ferry tourists and their cars between England and France. Using gas turbines to provide the air-cushion and turn their four large pusher propellers, SRN-4s can make the crossing in less than an hour.

The hull of an ACV does not touch the surface it is moving over, though the skirt can brush against it. If the surface is fairly smooth, it does not matter whether it is water, land or swamp.

Hovercraft have, for this reason, been used by explorers in South America and Africa. But rough water or long, steep slopes can get a hovercraft into difficulties. There are other drawbacks. A hovercraft's propellers make it as noisy as a plane. Its engines are costly to make and to run. As it needs to be strong but light, a hovercraft is expensive to build. However, research is being carried out to find solutions to these problems.

Advances made by scientists may mean that the ACV of the future will be the hovertrain. In several countries, experiments have recently been made with electric rail-cars travelling at high speed, less than a centimetre above a fixed track.

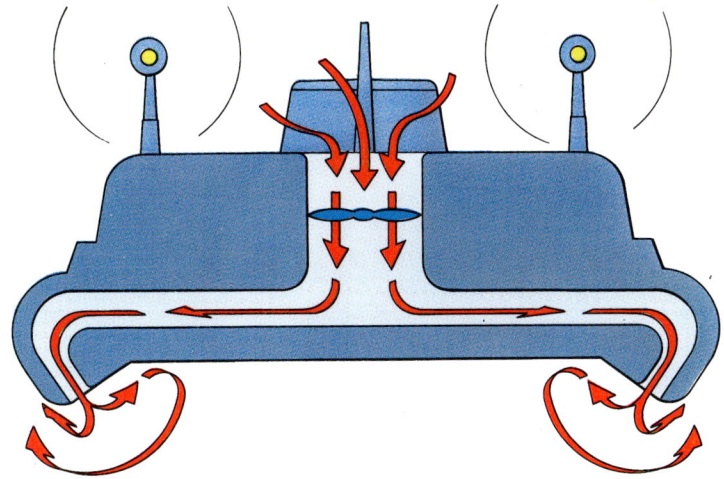

The air is forced down into the chamber by powerful fans. Forward movement comes from aircraft-type propellers that can be turned in different directions to enable the craft to be steered.

The AP.1-88 hovercraft is used in a wide variety of commercial and military roles. As a passenger ferry it can seat up to one hundred passengers. It is also used for search and rescue, geographical surveying, anti-smuggling operations and fire-fighting.

Transport and machines for the handicapped

MANY DISABLED PEOPLE need help to overcome the difficulties of everyday life. Their major problems are numerous. One of these is moving about, both inside their homes and outside. Many of these handicapped people have difficulty with reaching up high or with stooping down low. Some manage with little or no assistance. Others need continual help.

Nowadays, many mechanical and electronic aids are being used to help such people overcome their handicaps and cope more easily by themselves. Computers have been used for a long time to control machinery in factories. Recently it has become possible to make very small computers called **microcomputers**. These are used in pocket calculators, video games and digital watches. Machines using this new technology are now being made to help disabled people lead more normal lives.

Disabled people often find difficulty in getting around. A physically handicapped person may own a wheelchair. A severely handicapped person may find power-assisted steering essential. This is because they have little strength to steer themselves. Chairs can be operated by single levers controlled by a finger, movement of a toe, or even by a suck-and-blow mechanism using the mouth. The controls may be mounted on one of the arm rests or on a steering column between the user's legs.

Powered wheelchairs may sometimes be folded and carried in a car. However, they are

This vehicle is a specially designed car for the chairbound. Its large rear door allows easy access up a small ramp. Once inside, the wheelchair is locked into the driving position. The controls are hand operated and can be adjusted to suit the individual.

larger than the older hand-operated ones. Some vehicles are fitted with a special hoist to help a disabled person get both the wheelchair and himself inside. Most road vehicles can be adapted for use by a disabled driver. Cars with automatic transmission are easier for them to drive. Some vehicles are modified to have either all hand-operated controls, all foot-operated controls, or one-hand and one-leg controls. Special types of handles are often fitted to the controls of the car to make them easier to hold or reach.

Blind people have traditionally used guide dogs or a white stick to help them in their travels. Many are so skilful at this that movement poses few major problems for them. However, the white stick may one day be replaced by electronic devices that produce an audible signal which the blind person can use to move about safely and avoid obstructions. These devices enable people to navigate in much the same way that bats do – by sensing their surroundings, using sound waves. However, such equipment is difficult to use, and full training is necessary.

Handicapped people may not be able to see, hear or speak properly. Blind people have been able to read for over one hundred years, thanks to a blind Frenchman named Louis Braille. He invented a system of raised dots which could be felt with the fingers. This enabled the letters of

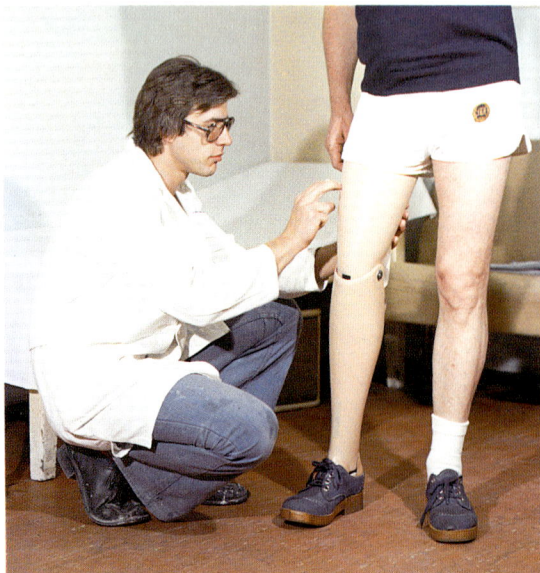

Fitting of artificial limbs is an involved procedure since they have to be tailor-made. In this case the patient has to be assisted with learning to walk using the new leg, at first with the aid of sticks and eventually completely unaided. The jointed limb is designed to match the behaviour of a real limb as closely as possible.

the alphabet to be recognized. Various instruments are available that allow blind people to type Braille patterns on to paper.

New machines now enable ordinary books and letters to be read by the blind without first being translated into Braille. The OPTACON machine produces the shapes of printed letters, appearing under a camera, on a number of vibrating pins. A speaking attachment is also available. This produces a spoken word output as the camera is moved across a page. There is a great need for machines that talk. Small computer-controlled speech units are now added to electronic calculators, the keypads of modern telephones, telephone switchboards and even typewriters.

Typewriters no longer have to be controlled just by the fingertips. Physically handicapped people often have little use of their hands. A

An OPTACON machine in use *(right)*. OPTACON stands for OPtical TACtile CONvertor; a small lens and camera are held in one hand and moved across the printed page. The other hand is placed with the index finger in a groove under which are vibrating pins.

breath-controlled typewriter uses a special mouthpiece to select the letters which the user wants to type. Blowing again then types the letter. Modern electronics have made this sort of typewriter far easier to use. A whole line of type may be stored in a computer memory. This can be corrected if necessary, and then printed a line at a time. A tidy, well laid out copy is produced. Some handicapped people are able to type at a computer terminal using either their nose or their feet, instead of their fingers. In addition to typing, they are able to write computer programs. These are the series of commands which tell computers exactly what to do.

Subtitles for those with hearing difficulties have been a common sight on television news programmes for some years. By means of Teletext, pages of news, weather, travel, recipes and

(above) Children with hearing difficulties have to keep pace with other children in all aspects of education. It is now possible, with modern electronic aids, for the handicapped child to be educated in a normal classroom, provided the teachers have special training. In some cases, where there is a partially deaf child in a class, the teacher carries a transmitter and the child has a receiver. This way, the handicapped child can take part in normal classes.

Computers can help the severely handicapped perform many everyday tasks such as switching on lights, or answering the telephone. They are also used as learning aids.

other information are available on a television screen. Teletext is a great help to the deaf, and disabled or elderly people who cannot get out of the house. Deaf people often have great difficulty taking part in conversation. A deaf person may lip-read one speaker. However, if several people are talking together, details may be missed. Hearing aids have been available for many years. Now the new developments in electronics mean that hearing aids can be made smaller and more complicated. They are also more reliable. Recently, speech recognition computers have become available. These can recognize spoken words and display them on a screen. Unfortunately, the recognition process is at present rather slow. In a few years' time it should also be possible to display a visual record of rapid conversation. This will be of great benefit to deaf people.

Factory automation

THROUGHOUT HISTORY, humans have built machines to do their work for them. **Machine tools** are machines that have been used to make the parts for yet more machines. There are many types of machine tools. The simplest are drilling machines, which are used for making holes, the grinders which smooth down surfaces to the required thickness or smoothness, and the presses which cut out various shapes from sheets of material. Then there are lathes. These machines shape pieces of wood or metal by rotating (turning) them against a cutting tool. A milling machine is used for cutting grooves or slots, and a shaper is used for fashioning a piece of material into a desired figure or form.

Until recently, all these machine tools had a human operator to control them. However, many machining jobs in factories are extremely boring and repetitive. The same task is carried out countless times, day after day. Often, the jobs are dirty and unpleasant, and sometimes even dangerous. For this reason, many factories are now using electronic computers for the automatic control of machinery. The computer may perform only a simple task, but, once its program of instructions has been written, it will do the same job as many times as is required. Providing they do not break down, automatic machines can work continuously, day or night, on every day of the year. The computer-con-

A fully-automated production line *(above)* controlled by a central computer. At each stage robots can perform a variety of tasks. *(below)* A traditional engineering works. Jobs like those of these lathe operators are now carried out by machines

trolled machines are often called CNC machine tools. The initials stand for Computer Numerical Control.

At one time, the breakdown of some small machine or a power cut might have shut down a whole production plant. Nowadays, the number of stoppages due to breakdown of essential equipment has been reduced. Machines are often provided with a special computer system which automatically checks every working part. This gives a warning if a breakdown is likely. A spare machine may then be brought in quickly to fill the gap. Production may continue while an engineer finds out what is wrong. This procedure is called 'condition' monitoring, or 'health' monitoring. It greatly reduces the number of stoppages in a manufacturing process. Some computers check themselves, and look for faulty power supplies or electronic circuits. If one is detected, the computer may automatically switch in a 'back-up' circuit, and summon an electronics engineer, telling him exactly what part needs replacing.

In any manufacturing process, cost must be kept as low as possible, This has been achieved by **mass production**. Many thousands of com-

ponents, or parts, all exactly the same, are produced one after another by the same machines. The setting up and adjustment of a machine tool may take several hours. Because of this, it is very wasteful of time and money to keep changing these settings. A machine will be used to mass produce many thousands of components of one particular design before the machine settings are changed. As most of these components will not be needed straight away, they must be stored. However, the cost of each one is kept low.

In the last twenty years, by using CNC machine tools, it has become possible to make different parts in small batches, with the same machines. The cost is similar to that of mass production. This process has become known as

Summary of Terms

CNC	Computer Numerical Control
ASP	Automated Small-batch Production
FMS	Flexible Manufacturing System
AGV	Automatic Guided Vehicles

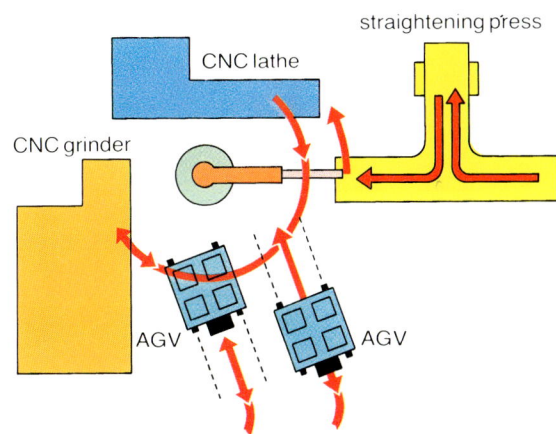

This robot *(below and left)* performs a demanding task. Its job is to pick up components that have been through a straightening press and place them in a grinder. Some components, which the robot has to recognize, need to be put into a second grinder. Once grinding is complete a signal tells the robot to load the component into a basket. These baskets are then removed by an AGV.

In an FMS cell, every machine tool, robot, conveyor or AGV is under computer control. Each CNC machine has its own computer, and the whole FMS cell will usually be under the overall control of one central computer, called the **system supervisor**. This controls all the other computers, and makes sure that every machine and robot is working properly. It also checks that machined parts move smoothly from one stage of the manufacturing process to the next. Timing is particularly important, as the work is carried out at high speed. The interesting thing about the FMS cell is that it can be easily and quickly re-programmed to manufacture a totally different part, because it is all under computer control.

A factory containing a number of FMS cells is never completely unmanned. As few as three, four or five people operate an FMS cell during the daytime. At night, only one or two people need be present. They attend to the machines if maintenance is necessary, and keep a check on the control and supervisory computers. Someone has to watch the computer screens, supervise the loading of the blanks, and the removal of the finished parts. The totally unmanned factory lies in the future. However, there is no doubt that fewer and fewer of us will be employed to do dirty and tedious manual work on production lines in factories, in the coming years.

Automated Small-batch Production, or **ASP** for short. Nowadays, even more complex methods of making components in factories are being introduced. These so-called 'factories of the future' have their machine tools grouped together into what are known as **FMS cells**. The letters FMS stand for **F**lexible **M**anufacturing **S**ystem.

An FMS cell consists of a number of CNC machine tools. These machines are supplied with metal components, called 'blanks', which are carried either on moving conveyor belts, or by special **A**utomatic **G**uided **V**ehicles, known as **AGV**s. As the metal blanks arrive at the FMS cell, industrial **robots** lift the parts from the conveyor, or vehicle, on to the machine tools. Industrial robots are described elsewhere in this book. As each lathe, grinder or other CNC machine tool finishes its task, the metal part is lifted off by the robot and passed to the next machine in the FMS cell. In this way, each metal blank is steadily machined into the finished product by several machine tools. Finally, a robot lifts completed parts on to another vehicle or conveyor. They will then be taken elsewhere in the factory for immediate use or storage.

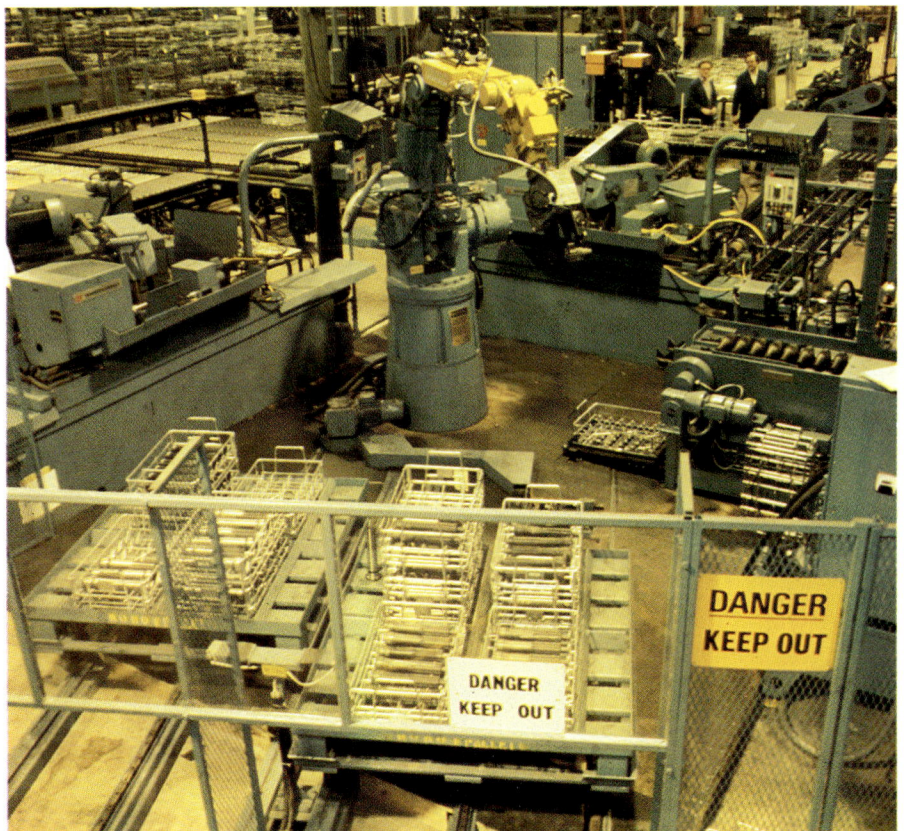

The first generation of robots

THE WORD **robot** was first used by a Czechoslovakian playwright in 1923. For most people, it conjures up a picture of a complicated machine, which looks very much like a human being. It would be very strong and, usually, able to talk and walk. Science fiction writers of both books and films have done much to popularize this view of highly intelligent robots. However, real robots are very different. The majority of robots in factories do not look at all like those in science fiction stories. Modern robots are quite often mechanical arms, controlled by computers. The robot is a machine that can be programmed to do different tasks. Nowadays, more and more robots are being put to work in factories throughout the world. These **industrial robots**, as they are called, are being used for a wide variety of jobs. They may weld things together, spray paint, spread glue on surfaces, or load and unload engineering parts from conveyor systems or vehicles.

To get an idea of what a typical industrial robot can do, imagine a blindfolded human worker tied to a chair and able only to move one arm, and to twist at the waist. If you look at your own arm you will see that it has joints at the shoulder, elbow and wrist. Robots have joints too. In a robot, each joint is called a **degree of freedom**. Most industrial robots have five or six

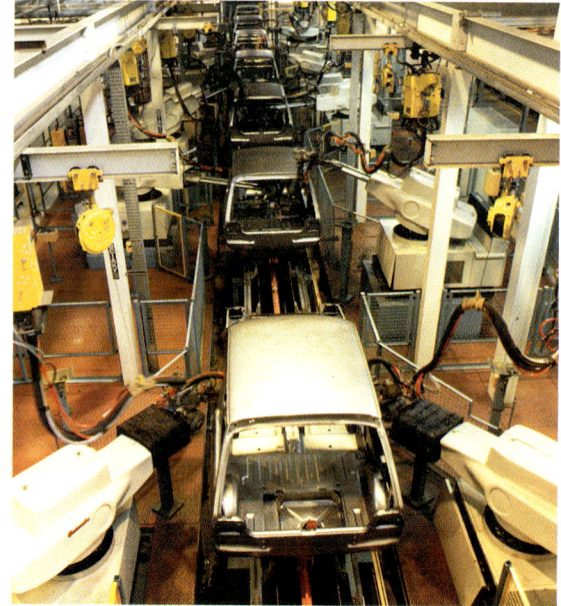

This car production line is controlled by a central computer. Robots here are being used to weld body shells as they pass down the line.

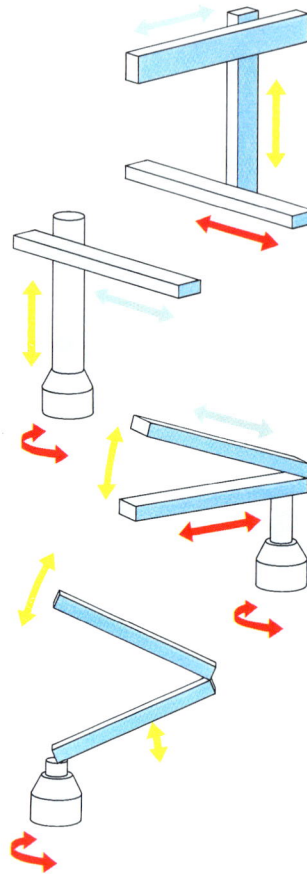

The range of movement in four different types of robots. Yellow arrows indicate elevation, green show reach, and red, travel or rotation. This range is known as degrees of freedom.

Repetitive jobs are ideally suited to robots because they can perform the same task without a break for twenty-four hours a day. This robot is loading finished products into packing cases at the end of a production line.

degrees of freedom. A typical robot is able to rotate on its base through almost a full circle, similar to a human twisting at the waist. The robot arm might also have joints which correspond to the shoulder, elbow and wrist in human beings.

A robot's wrist may have up to three degrees of freedom, although many robots have only two. At the end of the wrist is the robot **gripper** which holds its tools. This might be a welding torch, or a paint spray gun, for example. Grippers are often designed specially for the job which the robot is to carry out. Some robots can automatically change their gripper during operation. The opening and closing of a gripper is usually done pneumatically. The word **pneumatic** means that the movement is controlled by high-pressure air pushing a piston.

The size of a robot usually depends on how much weight it can lift. A small robot might lift small loads of up to 10 kg. Larger robots can lift from 60 to 100 kg, and a few can manage considerably more than this. It is important to know how far a robot can reach in any direction around it, and how fast it can move. Typical industrial robots have an arm which can reach a distance of 2 metres. The speed of movement is about 1.5 metres per second. It is also important for the robot to be programmed to move the load from one place to another very accurately. This

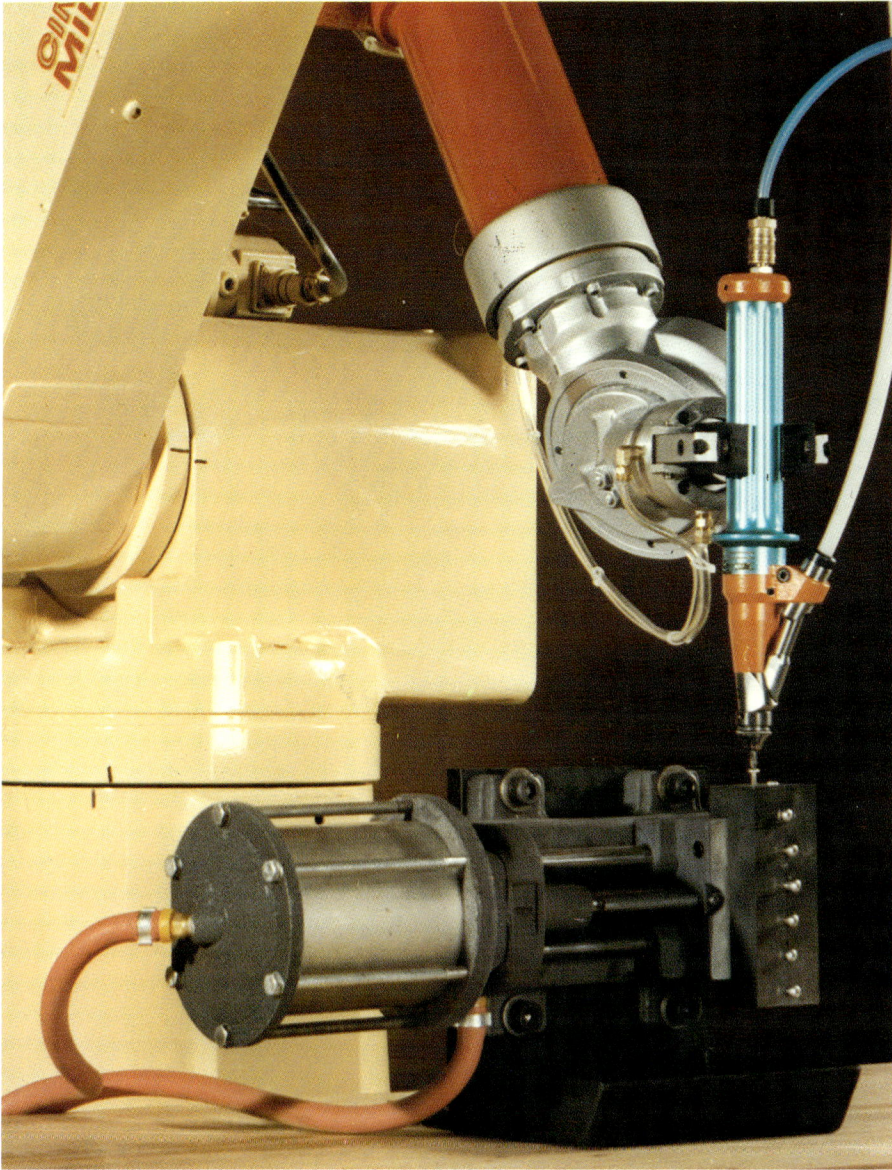

robot. The tool must go to these positions, in order to do its job. This might be picking up a part from a cart, loading a machine tool, or doing spot welding on the body of a car. The computer which controls the robot then makes it move between these set points. It goes from one to the next, in sequence. This movement is usually in a fairly straight line. With this method, the motion appears as a series of short, separate movements and not a smooth path.

Sometimes, a much smoother movement is needed, as, for example, in paint spraying. Here, continuous path motion is needed. This means that the robot has to be programmed with the actual path it must follow, and the variations in speed along that path. This method of programming is more complicated. For many simple **pick-and-place** tasks, point-to-point motion is quite adequate. It is also possible to program a robot movement as a series of set points, but then to have the computer calculate a smooth curve which passes through all of them. The robot will then be made to move along the calculated curve. This method is easier to program than continuous path moves.

Once a given series of movements has been fed into the robot, it will perform the required tasks. It will go on doing this for twenty-four hours a day if necessary. Robots do not get tired or bored. They can work in dangerous, hot, noisy and dirty places, which are extremely unpleasant or, indeed, impossible for humans. The jobs that robots carry out are, normally, the highly repetitive ones on production lines in factories. Robots are widely used in the handling of chemicals and engineering parts. They are also used in the manufacture of all kinds of goods from cars, washing machines and stoves, to clothing and foodstuffs. In the automobile industry, robots are now used at nearly every stage of production.

is called the **repeatability** of the robot. Many robots can position a load with a repeatability of only a fraction of a millimetre.

Each joint of a robot may be powered in one of three different ways. Some robots, which are designed to lift weights of up to 10 kg, are completely pneumatically-powered. Where great strength, but not precise repeatability is needed, robots are often hydraulically-powered. The word **hydraulic** means that the movement is controlled by high-pressure liquid pushing a piston. Finally, there are electrically-powered robots. These are the most accurate. Here, electric motors are used to power robots from the very smallest types to some of the largest.

Robots may be programmed to move in different ways. The most important of these ways are called **point-to-point** movement and **continuous path** motion. With point-to-point, a series of positions is programmed around the

Like humans, robots have jointed arms and wrists, to provide as much flexibility as possible. A robot's 'hand' can be programmed to hold a wide variety of objects and tools, large or small. Here a robot is using a screwdriver, operated by compressed air, to drive screws into a block.

A robot that sniffs? Here we see robots dry-leak testing, where they check for flaws in the doors, windows and seams that could cause water leaks. The interior of the vehicle is first injected with air and helium, after which the robots scan the seals to detect any escaping gas.

Robots with artificial intelligence

THE 'BRAIN' of any robot is the computer or computers which control it. All the electronics, including the computers, needed to control the movement of the robot's joints are contained in a cabinet called the **robot control system**. This is connected to the robot by a set of cables. It is located as far away from the robot as safety demands. Normally, the control system will contain several small computers, called **micro-computers**, one for each joint of the robot. These are themselves under the control of another, larger computer, called the system supervisor. This tells the computers controlling the joints exactly what to do and when to do it. The system supervisor also checks that what they are doing is correct. Let us see how this control system works.

At each joint in the robot, there are special devices called **position sensors**. These produce electrical signals which tell the computers controlling the joints the exact position of each joint. These also tell the computers at what speed and in which direction each joint is moving. When the control system has been programmed to do a given job, each computer checks the position of its joint. Next, it compares this position with the point to which the joint has been programmed to go. It then produces an **error signal**. The greater the distance

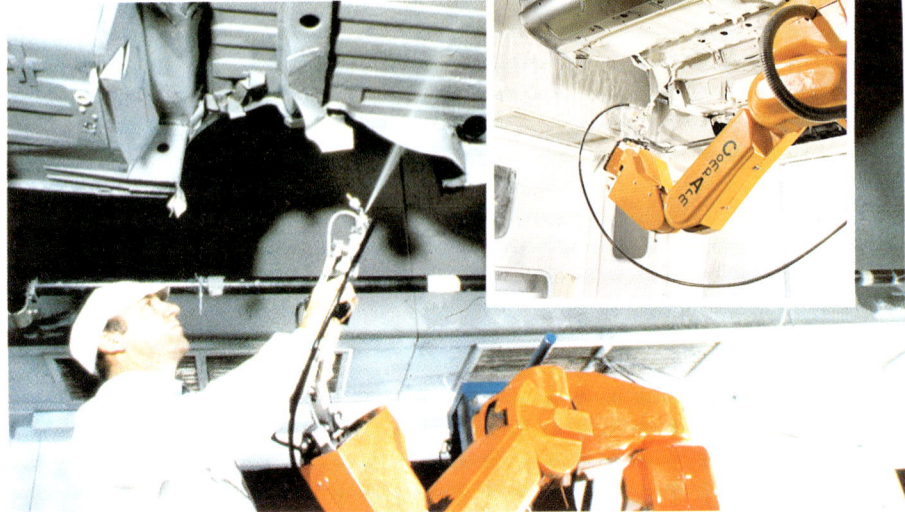

Programming a robot is known as teaching. In this case a man is showing a robot all the movements that it will need for its new job. These are recorded on the memory of the computer in the control system.

Spraying a complex object like this chair with paint or varnish is no easy job. Indication of the range of movements that the robot arm has to make, while keeping a uniform quality, is well shown in this multiple-image picture.

between the two positions, the longer the error signal. The motors are then activated to work to reduce this error signal. This causes movement of each joint in the required direction. The computer will also automatically speed up the movement of each joint to full speed, and then slow it down as it approaches the desired position. This makes sure that it does not overshoot.

The earliest, **first generation** robots possessed only position sensors on their joints. To carry out any task, they had to be taught exactly where and how each joint had to move. Teaching a robot involves programming all the movements required into the memory of the main computer in the control system. A robot is usually taught by the person who will supervise it, and who knows about the job the robot will do. Teaching may be achieved in several ways. The majority of teaching methods rely on the information which is fed back to the computer from the position sensors in the joints. In one method, a handle is fitted to the front of the robot. The robot is then taught by actually leading it through the sequence of moves it has to follow. This is like taking someone by the hand to show them the way in a strange place.

Future robots will be given all kinds of sensors. This will allow them to choose different courses of action depending on what is happening around them. A robot with a vision system could identify different items and pick them up in different ways. It could even be used to build a piece of machinery by fitting together a number of component parts. This is a process called **robot assembly**. For this sort of task, robots will be given a sense of touch, using complex electronic sensors. This will keep them from damaging fragile objects by gripping them too hard, or dropping them by not gripping them hard enough. However, even fitted with sensors, very powerful computers will be needed to control a robot well enough to fit several metal parts together and perform assembly tasks. Robots might also be given a sense that humans do not possess. This is **proximity sensing**, which is knowing how close you are to an object without touching it. This would be particularly useful in preventing robots from colliding with people, other robots, or items of furniture or machinery.

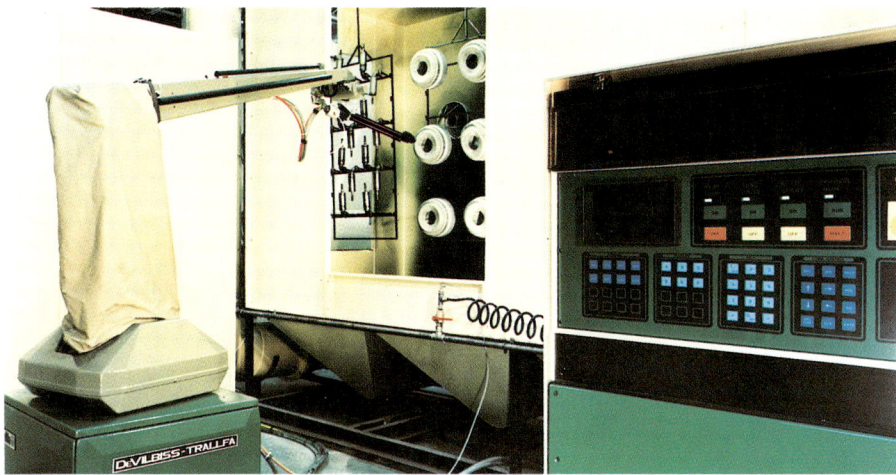

As the robot is moved about, it is possible to record positions into the computer memory by pushing a button or trigger on the robot arm.

The most common way of teaching a robot is by use of a **teach pendant**. This has buttons on it, or a joystick control, which the teacher uses to drive each of the robot's joints. The pendant is connected to the control system by a cable. The teacher slowly guides the robot arm in the required direction, using the pendant controls. As the arm moves from position to position, the teacher keeps pressing a record button on the pendant. This enters each position into the robot's computer memory. When the movements have been completed, the robot can then carry out the whole task on its own. Trial runs of the program may show some errors in the movement. In this case, small adjustments may be made, using the pendant. This is done until the movement is just right. A robot may be taught to do several completely different tasks. The program for each can be stored in the computer's memory. The robot can then come back to any of the jobs at any time.

The problem with the early first-generation robots is that they have no outside sensors. They cannot obtain any idea of what is around them. For example, suppose a robot was programmed to do a simple pick-and-place task like picking up a cup from a table. As long as the cup was always in the same place on the table, there would be no problem. However, if the cup was moved to one side, or taken away altogether, the robot would be unaware of the change. It would continue the same series of movements, without stopping, until it was switched off. What is needed is a robot with some form of **artificial intelligence**. We want the robot to be able to see, touch or feel its way about. Then it would be able to sense that we had moved the cup, and correct its movements to take account of the change.

Recent developments include sensor systems that bring the power of sight and brains to welding robots. The system (below) steers itself along an irregular joint, observing the weld and making any necessary adjustments as it travels along.

Summary

Throughout this book we have seen how humans have built more and more complicated tools and machines to help do their work. Throughout history, there have been several industrial revolutions, during which machines have been developed at great speed. It started with the engineers in Egypt and Mesopotamia, who used simple pulleys and levers. Later the Greek scientists and Roman engineers developed these machines a stage further. They found yet more ways of applying their ingenuity to do the jobs that had to be done at that time. In the early eighteenth century there was the start of the greatest Industrial Revolution. This led in a short space of time to the first true engines. It also led to the development of automated factory machinery and the beginning of steam power and railways.

Machines are not always welcomed by the people needed to operate them. In 1811, at a time of great poverty in England, a group of workmen decided that the cause of their troubles was the new factory machinery. This was being used to produce cloth, a major industry of the period. They became known as the *Luddites*. Their aim was to destroy as many of the new machines as possible. Riots took place in many parts of England. Many people were

The machines that have arguably transformed our world more than any other are computers. They are increasingly being used in navigation and communication systems. This computerised fire service control room ensures the quickest possible response to alarm calls.

An artist's impression of a space station of the future. This is planned to go into operation before the year 2000.

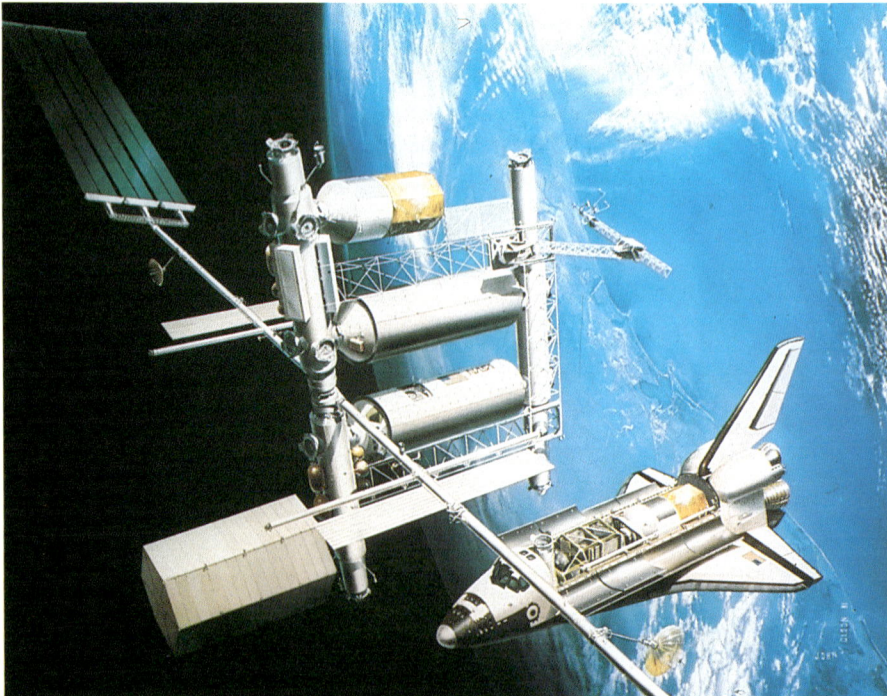

killed and large quantities of machinery were destroyed. However, the *Luddites* could not stop the introduction of the new machines. The factory owners saw that the machines worked faster than humans. They could also produce goods more cheaply than those which were hand-made. There has often been suspicion and worry about the effect that new machines would have on employment. This is also true today. For example, the widespread introduction of industrial robots has caused much concern.

It is probably true to say that the twentieth century has seen the greatest technological revolution in the history of mankind. The most important changes have been in transportation and communications. We have seen the development from the first propeller aircraft to jet engines and, later, rockets. These rockets have propelled astronauts to the Moon, our nearest neighbour in space. They have sent space probes to other planets. Cars, too, have undergone dramatic changes since their invention, and ships have progressed to hydrofoils and hovercraft. In communications, we have seen the invention of radio, television and modern electronic computers. Using a network of **satellites** orbiting high above the Earth's surface, messages may be sent across the world. There are now millions of telephones worldwide. Messages can be sent at the push of a button.

This cutting laser is being controlled by a computer. It is removing small pieces of metal from a turbine rotor in order to balance it. By hand this job would take a skilled engineer a very long time, while the laser performs the task in a few minutes.

The electrically-powered bullet trains of Japan (below) can cruise at 209kph. Those of the future, however, are likely to be different. 'Maglev' trains, supported over the track by magnetic forces, not wheels, have already travelled at over 500kph.

Without doubt, the 1980s and 1990s will see yet another stage in this great revolution in the use of machines. Robots will be increasingly used in factories and in industry. By the year 2000, robots may be used to build still more robots. The space probes which have landed on Venus and Mars, and swooped past Jupiter and Saturn, are some of the most sophisticated robot craft ever built. In the future, we shall see increasing use of robots in space. They will be employed to build space stations and construct massive solar panels. These will collect the Sun's rays. Perhaps the solar energy collected will be beamed down to the Earth's surface as **microwaves**. Perhaps robots will be sent to the Moon to mine rare metals or minerals which have become in short supply on Earth.

The revolution in transportation will continue. It is unlikely that very fast planes such as the Concorde will become common. This is because fuel resources will decrease. Some major developments will be necessary. It may be that some completely new forms of propulsion will be found both for space travel and for aircraft. As long as the car is powered by a petrol engine, it will be doomed to extinction. The air **pollution** caused by cars, and the rising prices of oil and petrol will be their downfall. In the future, cars may be banned from all inner cities, where poisonous fumes and traffic congestion are becoming a major problem. Electrically-powered metro-trains, called **Rapid Transit Systems**, driven entirely by robots, could ferry commuters into the inner cities. Electric vehicles are becoming more common. In the next twenty years their use may increase. New types of batteries and battery chargers will be developed for use in electric vehicles.

As the world becomes more automated, and robots become more widely used, unemployment will probably rise unless staff retraining occurs. There will be a great need for people to make better use of their leisure time, because they will spend less time at work. When every home has its own computer, many office workers will not need to travel into work. They will be able to do all their work at home and communicate with the office computer whenever necessary.

Glossary

aerodynamics: the study of the flow of air and gases.

aerofoil: a wing, *rudder*, tail-plane, or anything shaped to produce *lift* when air flows over and under it.

AGV (Automatic Guided Vehicle): a vehicle driven by computer, used in factories to carry materials to and from the machines.

aileron: a flap at the rear edge of each aircraft wing, which the pilot raises or lowers to keep the craft steady or change direction.

air cushion vehicle: a vehicle, such as a hovercraft, supported above land or water by a layer of air.

aqueduct: a pipe or channel built to carry flowing water.

Archimedes' screw: a pipe wound in the form of a screw with its lower end in water. When turned, it raises the water to a higher level.

artificial intelligence: the ability of a *robot* to find out what is happening around it, using sensors, and then to change its actions depending on what it has discovered.

ASP (Automated Small-batch Production): using a single machine to make different machine parts in small numbers, by means of computerized *machine tools*.

atmospheric engine: one partly driven by air pressure.

axle: the shaft under the vehicle to which its wheels are attached.

ball race: one of the grooved walls around a ball-bearing in which steel balls roll to help a wheel turn freely.

banking: turning an aircraft in flight, by tilting it to one side, using the *ailerons*.

Bernouilli effect: the effect of *lift* produced by the lowering of air pressure over an *aerofoil*.

bicycle: a vehicle with two wheels, driven by pedals.

bobbin: a reel or spool on to which thread is wound for weaving or machine sewing.

bogie: a set of wheels at the front of a railway engine, which turns on a pivot under the engine and makes it more stable going round bends.

cam: a wheel flattened on one side, used to raise and lower a beam in order to change circular movement into up-and-down movement.

camber: the curve of a surface, such as an *aerofoil*.

canopy: the fabric part of a parachute under which air is trapped.

capstan: an upright winding machine used to haul heavy objects by rope or cable. It is turned by pushing on a bar attached to the top.

cereal: any kind of grain, such as rice or oats, that can be used as food.

chainwheel: a wheel with teeth that fit into the links of a chain running around its edge. When it is turned the chain will move to turn a second wheel.

civilization: a large, organized community of people who have developed their own language, customs, laws, trade, and so on.

compress: to squash something into a smaller space.

compressor: part of a gas turbine or jet engine in which air is put under high pressure.

condense: to turn from a gas or vapour into a liquid, by cooling.

condenser: a container in which steam from the *cylinder* of a steam engine is cooled to create a partial *vacuum*.

continuous path: the path of a *robot* which moves in order to carry out its task.

crankshaft: the main driving rod of an engine. It is turned by an arm which is attached to it and is connected to a piston.

cruising speed: in a machine such as a car, the speed that makes best use of the fuel and allows the engine to run easily.

cultivate: to prepare land to make it suitable for growing crops.

cyclic pitch: the way in which the *rotor-blades* of a helicopter change angle as they go round to tilt the rotor and send the helicopter forward.

cylinder: a solid or hollow tube with circular ends and parallel sides. In an engine it is the tube in which the *piston* moves.

degree of freedom: the amount of movement that can be made by each joint of a *robot*.

differential: in a car, the set of *gears* that converts the drive of the *propeller shaft* into that of the back wheels, and allows the wheels to turn independently when the car is cornering.

dirigible: able to be directed, or steered.

drag: resistance to motion through a gas or liquid.

effort: the *force* needed to do a piece of work.

ejector seat: a seat that can be shot clear of an aircraft, with a person sitting in it, in an emergency.

electromagnet: an iron bar surrounded by a coil of wire that behaves as a magnet when an electric current flows through the wire.

elevator: a movable blade on an aircraft, used to steer it up or down in the air.

engine torque: the tendency of a helicopter to turn in the opposite direction to that in which the *rotor-blades* are spinning.

environment: the surroundings of any animal or plant.

error signal: a signal given by a computer controlling a *robot* joint to start the motors that move it to the correct position.

fertile: having soil in which plants will grow well.

fibre: a single, thin strand, or thread, of a material.

fin: a fixed blade on an aircraft which keeps it steady.

first generation: the first range of models of a new invention.

flange: a raised edge, such as the rim of a railway wheel.

flap: a surface attached to the rear edge of an aircraft's wing which can be lowered to increase the *lift*.

flint: a hard rock that can be chipped away to produce a sharp edge. It was used to make tools by early people who had not yet discovered how to use metals.

flywheel: a large, heavy wheel attached to the *crankshaft* of an engine which helps to keep its speed steady.

FMS (Flexible Manufacturing System) cell: a group of computerized *machine tools*, each carrying out a different job, that can make a whole machine part automatically.

force: the energy needed to change the direction or speed of a body that is free to move.

friction: the *drag* caused by two surfaces rubbing together, which produces heat, wear, and an electric charge.

fuselage: the main body of an aircraft.

gear: a way of using toothed wheels to drive each other round and convey movement from one part of a machine to another. In a car, each gear changes the high spinning speed of the *crankshaft* to a lower speed to drive the car's wheels.

gradient: slope

gravity: the natural pulling force exerted by any large mass, for example the Earth.

gripper: a *robot*'s 'hand', which it uses to hold a tool or pick something up.

groma: a Roman instrument for surveying land when planning new roads.

half-shaft: in a car, the shaft that carries one driving wheel so that it can turn independently of the wheel on the other side when cornering.

hang-glider: a very small glider, usually launched from a hillside.

harness: the system of electrical wiring that runs round a car to provide power for ignition, lights, etc.

helium: a very stable gas, made from hydrogen at very high temperatures. It is found in small quantities in the atmosphere.

hemisphere: one half of a sphere, or ball.

hemp: the general name for a number of different plant fibres used for making rope and matting.

hydraulic: operated by the force of compressed liquid.

industrial robot: a *robot* programmed to do a routine job in a factory.

internal combustion engine: an engine in which fuel burns inside a *cylinder* to drive a *piston*. The engine may have one or more cylinders.

irrigate: to provide water for growing crops.

kerosine: a fuel made from petroleum, used to provide the power for jet engines.

lathe: a *machine tool* used to shape cylindrical parts such as *pistons*.

lever: a simple *machine* for lifting loads, consisting of a rigid beam turning on a *pivot*, like a seesaw.

lift: the *force*, created by the difference in air pressure above and below the wings, which keeps an aircraft in flight.

loom: a machine used for weaving cloth, originally just a frame to hold the *warp*.

machine: any artificial device that enables its operator to use less *effort* to do a piece of work.

machine tool: a power-driven machine used to shape parts of other machines, usually in metal.

manoeuvre: to change position and direction.

mass production: using a machine to make thousands, or millions, of identical articles, to keep the cost of each one low.

mechanical advantage: the relation between the amount of work done by a machine and the *effort* needed.

microcomputer: a small computer containing a microprocessor which may be used to control simple robot operations.

microwave: a very high frequency radio wave.

mortar: a stone bowl used to hold grain being pounded with a *pestle* to make flour.

mule: a machine for spinning fine cotton thread, worked by water power.

obelisk: a tall stone pillar with four sides, narrowing to a point at the top, usually put up as a memorial.

overshot: describes a type of water-wheel in which the water flows over the wheel to turn it.

papyrus: a tall, reedy plant used in ancient Egypt to make boats, or, beaten out, to make sheets of paper.

patent: a licence obtained by the inventor or maker of a machine to stop anyone else using the same idea without permission and payment.

pestle: a blunt, stone tool used for pounding in a *mortar*.

pick-and-place: a simple job done by a *robot*, consisting of picking up, carrying, and putting down an object.

piston: a piece of metal which fits inside a *cylinder* and moves up and down. It may act as a pump or be pushed by a liquid or gas to produce power.

pitch: the angle between the blade of a propeller or a rotor and the horizontal.

pitch angle: the angle at which each propeller blade is set so that the propeller will move forward through water or air.

pivot: the pin on which a *lever* turns. The word also described the action of turning.

pneumatic: (*i*) filled with compressed air, like a balloon; (*ii*) operated by the force of compressed air in a cylinder.

point-to-point: the path of a *robot* which moves from one spot to another, stopping to do each job.

pollution: the act of making the *environment* dirty and harmful with rubbish, fumes and waste chemicals.

position sensor: an instrument in each joint of a *robot* which signals the joint's position, and how it is moving, back to the computer in control.

precision engineering: making objects, such as machine parts, to very accurate measurements.

program: a set of instructions given to a computer to enable it to carry out a task.

propeller shaft: the driving shaft which carries engine power in a car from the gearbox to the back *axle* to drive the wheels.

proximity sensing: the ability to find out how near an object is without touching it.

pulley: a wheel turning on a shaft that winds a rope or chain.

rack: a row of metal teeth along which a toothed wheel can travel without slipping.

Rapid Transit System: a network of fast trains usually powered by electricity.

reaction: a response to an action in the opposite direction.

reciprocating engine: an engine with a *piston* that is moved up and down in a *cylinder* by steam pressure.

repeatability: the way in which a *robot* is able to do the same job again and again in exactly the same way, or to carry objects to exactly the same place.

revolution: a complete circular turn by an object around its axis, back to its starting position.

robot: a machine that can do tasks automatically, once it has been programmed.

robot assembly: building a whole piece of machinery using one *robot* that does a series of different jobs.

robot control system: the computers and other electronics that control a *robot*.

rotary: going around and around

rotor-blades: the wings of a helicopter, which lift it by turning in a circle.

rudder: a vertical flap at the back of an aircraft or boat that can be moved to steer left or right.

satellite: a body in orbit around a larger body in space. Artificial satellites circling Earth reflect radio signals from one part of the world to another.

scaffolding: a structure of beams and platforms, put up for builders to work from and taken away when the building is finished.

spindle: a pin, or bobbin, used to twist *fibres* into thread, on to which the thread is wound as it is made.

sprocket: a small *chainwheel*, turned by the moving chain.

stall: an aircraft stalls if its wings are tilted too steeply in the air, or if it is moving too slowly; the effect of *lift* is upset and can no longer keep it airborne.

system supervisor: the central computer that controls all the sections of an *FMS cell* through each of their computers.

teach pendant: an instrument used to drive the joints of a *robot* while it is being programmed.

technology: putting scientific discoveries to practical or industrial uses.

tension: a strain produced by pulling or stretching.

thermal: a current of air that is rising because it has been heated.

throw: to form a piece of pottery from clay turning on a horizontal wheel.

thrust: power to move forward.

traction engine: a steam engine with very large wheels, designed to pull heavy loads on roads.

transmission: the system in a car that carries power from the engine to the revolving *axle* to which the driving wheels are fixed.

undershot: describes a type of water-wheel in which the water turns the wheel by flowing under it.

vacuum: an empty space with no air or any other matter in it.

valve: an instrument that controls the direction and speed of a fluid (such as water, air or steam) flowing along a channel.

variometer: an instrument that shows how fast a glider is climbing or falling in the air.

velocipede: an early type of *bicycle* with pedals fixed to the front wheel.

warp: the vertical threads wound on to the *loom* through which the *weft* is passed when weaving cloth.

weft: the crosswise threads passed over and under the *warp* in weaving.

wheel housings: the spaces under the body of a car into which the wheels fit.

winch: a mechanism for hoisting something by connecting it to a cable which is then wound in around a drum.

windlass: a roller resting on supports, used for winding rope to haul heavy objects.

Index